Good Deals & Smart Steals

Good Housekeeping

Good Deals & Smart Steals

$AVE MONEY ON EVERYTHING!

Susan Randol

HEARST BOOKS

A division of Sterling Publishing Co., Inc.

New York / London
www.sterlingpublishing.com

contents

part 1: how to be a smart shopper 8

introduction

Life seems to get more expensive every day! Whether you're experiencing sticker shock at the grocery store or gasping at your utility bill, you can't help but wonder how every price you encounter could climb so high. Wouldn't it be nice instead to save money each time you opened your wallet?

Here is the handbook you need. *Good Housekeeping Good Deals & Smart Steals* is bursting with vital information on how to save money on every purchase—from clothes to groceries to phone service to television sets. It arms you with proven strategies for buying everything from a light bulb to a washing machine.

But don't think that planning ways to save money means lowering your standards or denying yourself necessary items. Instead, it's simply about getting what you want for less. With the advice in this book, a determination to save your hard-earned money, and a little extra effort, you can live handsomely on a scaled-down budget.

PART 1: How to Be a Smart Shopper takes you through the general ins and outs of budget-conscious shopping. You'll learn coupon strategies for almost anything you buy, how to use rebates and rewards programs, smart ways to shop online, and even techniques for shopping at yard sales, flea markets, and auctions. Then you can apply this knowledge to the advice in **PART 2: Get a Good Deal** and save big-time on purchases large and small. Organized by subject—furniture, electronics, shoes, and so on—these proven, easy-to-implement money-saving tips are designed for real people with busy lives.

Best of all, the information on these pages comes from the experts at the Good Housekeeping Research Institute. For more than 100 years, the Good Housekeeping Research Institute has evaluated household products, offered helpful advice, and championed the rights of consumers. It is also the driving force behind the Good Housekeeping Seal, the trusted icon awarded to products with a limited warranty from the Good Housekeeping Research Institute.

Whether you live on a tight budget, want to cut back on expenses, or simply love a bargain, *Good Housekeeping Good Deals & Smart Steals* is an invaluable resource that will pay for itself many times over.

—Miriam Arond, Director
The Good Housekeeping Research Institute

PART 1

HOW TO BE A SMART SHOPPER

Smart shoppers live by some basic rules to save money. They **plan ahead**—for this week's dinner menus, when replacing a toaster oven, or when buying sheets. They **wait for sales**. They **keep receipts** so they can easily return items. They **avoid paying credit card interest**. They **comparison-shop**. They take advantage of **savings opportunities**, such as coupons, senior discounts, and employee benefits ranging from free museum admissions to cell phone plan deals.

These and other strategies explained in Part 1 apply to almost every shopping situation you encounter. **How to be a Smart Shopper** shows you exactly how to comparison shop (in stores, with sales flyers, and online) as well as how to use coupons to your best advantage—even to the point of getting something for nothing! You'll learn the best places and times to shop, and how to negotiate for the best deal. So check out the information that follows, and use it every time you buy something.

coupons

Coupons have come a long way from the days when they saved you only a few pennies on products you wouldn't normally buy. Now you can find big-time savings on everything from staples at the grocery store to meals at a favorite restaurant to a comforter at your housewares store to shoes online. And when you know where to look for the best coupons and how to redeem them, you're looking at substantial savings.

where can you find the best coupons for groceries?

- Check out the coupon circulars in your weekend newspapers. They're chock-full of money-saving deals—there are often about 100 coupons in the inserts in Sunday's paper.

- Pull coupons from the little machines in grocery store aisles for additional savings.

- You can also find coupons pack-aged with your favorite products that may save you money on that particu-lar product (or even on an unrelated item that you may want) at checkout.

- Don't forget the Web. Not only can you find general Web sites that offer great savings—such as smartsource.com and valpak.com —you can also go to a particular  product's Web site and download coupons for items you know you'll buy. Online grocery shopping sites may let you use manufacturers' coupons and may even post special coupons for online customers.

where can you find coupons for other products and services?

- Many coupon Web sites let you search by product (or service) name, while others match your coupon search to your zip code so you know what's on sale where.

- If you're planning to shop at a specific store, check the store's Web site before you go. Sometimes store sites will post printable coupons that you can bring in for a discount.

- Search for etailer coupons online by going to Google and typing in "coupon codes" followed by the name of the Web site where you're shopping.

- When you're ready to buy something online, pay special attention during the checkout process. If the site asks for a coupon or promotion code, go to Google and see if you can track down a promotion code on a coupon Web site.

- Check out goodhousekeeping.com for coupons, codes, and bargains.

- Look for coupons sent with your credit card bills.

- In the mail you can find postcard-like coupons from local retailers as well as booklets and magazine-type publications with coupons for savings at pet stores, restaurants, fitness clubs, and more.

- Buy the Entertainment Book (entertainmentbook.com) if you plan to use a lot of its restaurant, travel, and entertainment coupons or one of its discounts for a large expense (a hotel stay, for example). You'll recoup the cost of the book in no time. Look at the coupons in the local edition of the book before you buy it to make sure you'll use them.

how can you best redeem grocery coupons?

- Shop at grocery stores that double the face value of your coupons—or even triple them. Look for promotions when stores that usually double them triple them.

- Star coupon items on your shopping list so you won't forget to use the coupons when you get to the store.

- Stock up on groceries at the end of the year when coupons are at their most plentiful. Food manufacturers issue more coupons just before the holidays in November and December than at any other time—and if you combine these coupons with holiday sales, you'll save a bundle.

- Get a double discount by matching your coupons to what's on sale each week at your grocery store.

- Apply the coupon with the largest value to the least expensive item possible; you'll be more likely to get more value for your money.

- Buy extra copies of the newspaper if it includes a high-value coupon for a nonperishable product you use frequently. Then use the multiple coupons over the coming weeks.

- Use coupons only for items you normally buy. Otherwise, you may end up with something you'll never use.

- Ask for a rain check if the coupon item is out of stock.

STAY ORGANIZED

Get a helpful coupon organizer—and no, a plastic bag doesn't qualify! You can buy a basic, plastic organizer at your grocery store or a more stylish version at a stationery store.

what's the best way to use coupons for nongrocery items?

- Trade coupons with friends, check out coupon-swapping bulletin boards at libraries and grocery stores, or trade coupons online.

- Stores that share a common owner may let you use coupons from one chain at a sister chain.

- Some stores honor their competitors' coupons—always ask about their policy.

- Find out if your local stores honor coupons that have expired. Some will accept coupons that are three months past their expiration date, while others honor coupons no matter when they expired.

BUYER BEWARE

Some stores honor coupons only on regularly-priced merchandise. If the item is on sale, your coupon may be applied to the item's original price, not to the sale price, thereby voiding all your savings. Watch the wording on the coupon.

rebates

Getting a rebate takes a little bit of work, but you can reap big rewards if you invest a small amount of time. Follow these steps to win the rebate game.

1 Keep an eye out for displays that advertise manufacturers' rebates or refunds. Check your sales slip too; often you'll find detailed rebate information there.

2 Get an extra store receipt. Keep an original receipt in your records—it'll come in handy if you need to track down or resubmit a claim. So ask for a duplicate when you buy.

3 Put your receipts in your purse, not in your shopping bag, to prevent their getting thrown away.

4 At home, clip the proof of purchase before you put a rebate product away. Then sit down and do the rebate paperwork immediately.

5 Read the fine print. Be sure you have your receipt, completed rebate form, UPC code, and anything else the offer requires. Make sure you follow the rebate instructions to the letter.

6 Write clearly. An illegible form is a common explanation for rejected rebates.

7 Photocopy the complete form before you send it in, in case the rebate doesn't arrive and you need to contact the manufacturer.

8 If you forgot to pick up a refund form in the store, check out the manufacturer's Web site *and* the store's Web site. You can sometimes find the forms you need and print them out.

9 Keep a list of rebates you sent in, with the numbers to call or Web sites to visit for information. Note how long the company says the rebate will take to arrive; check back if it doesn't show up. Note on your calendar the last date the rebate is due to you.

10 For high-value refunds, send the originals by registered mail (request a return receipt) well before the deadline. That way, you'll have proof you filed on time.

11 Some businesses let you track rebates online. So the next time you need to follow up on a rebate, find out if you can take the electronic route—it may save you time.

12 Complain. If you don't receive your check by the date specified in the offer, take action and contact the company (most rebate forms list a phone number or Web site). If that doesn't work, write to the Federal Trade Commission (ftc.gov), your state attorney general's office, and the Better Business Bureau (bbb.org), and send a copy to the company in question. It may speed up your payment.

AVOID COMMON REBATE FLUBS

Glossing over the fine print. Read instructions carefully to make sure you qualify for the rebate. Some companies, for example, won't send you a check unless you have a receipt proving that you also bought last year's model.

Forgetting attachments. Remember to send in the sales receipt, product bar code, rebate slip, and anything else the company requests. Staple all your paperwork together.

Missing a deadline. You might have as little as seven days to redeem your rebate, so try to get the filing done within the first two days of purchase.

Failing to keep a record. Copy your documents and mark on your calendar the date your check should arrive. By law, companies have to send your money back within the promised time frame. If it's late, visit the firm's Web site to find contact information for someone on the executive team, such as the vice president; going straight to the top may be more effective than calling customer service.

BEWARE OF REBATE SCAMS

If you're considering a purchase from an online store offering a rebate, be sure the site is prepared to handle any follow-up problems you may have. Check the store's contact page to see if a phone number and address are provided. If not, buy elsewhere.

Be wary of any rebate offer you may receive through an unsolicited e-mail. It could be an attempt to gain personal information.

For reliable rebates, check out ebates.com. Once you register at the free site, you can take advantage of hundreds of ongoing rebate programs.

stacking

Saving money at a store sale is great, but the way to save really big is by "stacking"—getting an even lower price by combining coupons, rebates, and other discounts. If that sounds like a lot of work, relax. Stacking is easier than ever thanks to stores' Web sites and marketing programs for loyal customers.

the basics

You can become a stacker by asking a store manager these questions:

1 Is there a mailing list or newsletter? (If so, enroll to get in on sales early.)

2 Where are coupons available?

3 Do you accept competitors' coupons, expired coupons, or multiple coupons?

4 Do you have a loyalty program? (These often let shoppers earn back cash or provide points that can be exchanged for a gift certificate or discount.)

5 Do you match competitors' prices?

6 Do you have a price-guarantee policy? (If the price drops within a specific period of time, stores with price guarantees will refund the difference.)

7 Do you offer rebates?

8 Do you participate in cash-back credit card programs such as Upromise?

stacking scenarios

Here's how this approach works for a few common purchases:

- Beauty and personal-care products. Use those "free after rebate" programs at drugstore chains such as CVS, Rite Aid, and Walgreens (you pay cash in the store and mail in the rebate, and the manufacturers reimburse you by check). Stack enough coupons and rebates, and you can make a profit! A savvy shopper bought $21 worth of "free after rebate" items at Walgreens, then saved $5.50 with coupons and got a $2 bonus by taking her rebate as a gift card. Net gain: $21 in free items and $7.50 in cash.

- Clothing. Many women's retailers issue coupons in their catalogs. Join their loyalty clubs and you'll get perks—like coupons for your birthday. For example, one shopper bought slacks and a jacket on sale at Chico's using a $25 catalog coupon, a $10 birthday coupon, and a 5 percent loyalty discount. Savings: $93—which was 57 percent off the $162 full price.

- Household items. Another shopper used six Bed Bath & Beyond coupons (each 20 percent off) to buy towels and washcloths on sale, and lopped off another 2 percent with her Upromise credit card. Total savings: $73— 61 percent below the original price.

negotiating

You know negotiating for a better price is perfectly acceptable—even expected—when buying a car or shopping at a tag sale. But you may not know that you can negotiate even in everyday shopping situations. According to Herb Cohen, author of *You Can Negotiate Anything*, the sticker price isn't always the final price; in fact, you'll find almost all prices have some wiggle room. Start by using these tips.

- Visit stores on weekday mornings, when retail traffic is slow.

- Think of yourself as a seller rather than as a buyer. Cohen says you need to understand that your *money*—not the product you want—is what's for sale.

- Bargain for things like free delivery or an extended warranty on electronics or a free accessory at a clothing store— above and beyond the negotiated price.

- Adopt what Cohen calls "a low-key pose of mild incompetence." In other words, act as though you really aren't sure you know what you're doing. Stand in front of the plasma TV you want and smile in a bewildered manner, mumbling, "Well, I'm not sure" to yourself as the salesperson arrives. When the salesperson—who will either tell you his name or have a name tag—asks if you like it and if it has the features you're looking for, respond with one syllable, hesitant answers. Once he quotes  you a price, reply (using his name) with "That's more than I can pay" or ask when the TV will be going on sale. Cohen says that the salesperson will lower the price right then and there, 90 percent of the time.

rewards programs

Do you shop at the same places day after day, stay at the same hotel chain on vacation, and use the same credit card when charging? If so, ask about their loyalty programs, which can reward you with free merchandise, free hotel upgrades or free nights, and free flights. Just be sure that the rewards aren't too small (buy twenty sweaters and get the next one free!) or too inconvenient (you can redeem your airline points on very few flights) that the value of the rewards program is no value at all. Here are the best ways to get the most out of your rewards programs.

retail

Loyalty programs are offered by just about every retail chain; many require very little paperwork to sign up. For example, Staples has let customers get 10 percent back on ink and toner, paper, and copying services if they're members of the Staples Rewards program.

Evaluate carefully the plans that charge annual fees. The $25 you might pay at Barnes & Noble to get 10 percent off on your purchases over the next year, for instance, makes sense if you'll spend more than $250 in that time frame.

credit cards

Use your credit cards to rack up points to redeem for airline miles, gift cards from a wide variety of retailers, restaurant

SPECIAL REWARDS

Register any credit or debit card with upromise.com, and then use that card when you shop to save money for college. Here's how it works: Use your card with a Upromise partner, and you'll get a percentage of your purchase credited to your college savings account. You can use your card with partner restaurants, retail stores, grocery stores, and drugstores as well as online. It even works if you buy certain brands at both participating and nonparticipating stores. Your friends and family can join the program and funnel their savings into your college savings account. You can also apply for a Upromise credit card, which gives you a percentage back on any purchases you make with that card.

meals, hotel stays, and even cash back. But use your credit cards wisely. Watch out for annual fees and high interest rates. In addition, you may find that some programs—often cards tied to retail stores—offer too little in return for having to spend too much.

Also, apply for credit cards cautiously. Your credit score can be negatively affected by opening too many new accounts. And canceling your credit cards—even unused cards—can also lower your credit score. Pay off your cards and either cut them up and dispose of them or put them away in a safe place.

hotels

Hotel loyalty programs generally reward you with upgrades to fancier rooms or free nights on future visits. Many hotel programs also let you redeem your points on car rentals, flights, and gift certificates. Beware of programs with points that expire quickly, with lots of blackout dates, or with rewards redeemed only on deluxe rooms, specific hotels, or when you pay full price.

online

Earn points online at mypoints.com, clickrewards.com, and greenpoints.com by shopping online, taking surveys, and visiting Web sites and then redeeming those points for gift certificates, merchandise, or discounts. Keep in mind that online programs ask for a lot of information in exchange for points, and you may be swamped with unwanted e-mail solicitations as a result. Also, make sure you can redeem your points *where* you want to redeem them.

airlines

There are many ways to rack up miles and fly for free:

- Eat at restaurants that award miles on your favorite airline.

- Get additional miles by booking your flights online.

- Use the credit card that awards you the most miles.

- Ask your phone company if it participates in a miles program.

- Rent a car and earn miles. You may even earn big-time miles when you buy a car.

- Send flowers through a company that awards miles.

- Use an airline-referred real estate agent to buy or sell a home.

- Get miles when you stay at airline-specified hotels.

- Take out a home equity loan and some lenders will add miles to your account.

- Pay for the additional miles you need to get a free flight.

car rental

Join a car rental loyalty program and get savings on future rentals, as well as faster reservations and the ability to choose a specific brand and model at select locations. Some rental car agencies also offer discounts on the rental of infant and child car seats and waive the fee for additional drivers.

online shopping

You know you can save money by shopping online, but you may not be sure what to do. You also want to have a pleasant, safe shopping experience. Here's how to have a rewarding online shopping trip.

web strategies

- Get cash rebates. One shopping portal, ebates.com, has links to hundreds of online retailers offering anywhere from 1 percent to 25 percent cash back each quarter.

- Save on shipping. Big chains like Circuit City allow customers to order online, then pick up the item at a nearby store. Sears lets you do the same thing for certain large items.

- Find designer deals. For example, shopittome.com lets you search more than 250 designer names by specific item: say, dresses or handbags. You'll then receive e-mails alerting you to sale items the site has culled from other online retailers specializing in name brands.

- Let Web sites compare prices for you. A number of them will tell you how much a certain item costs at different stores. Check out sites like bizrate.com, mysimon.com, shopping.com, and shopping.yahoo.com. In addition to prices, you'll often get information on delivery charges and customer-support services.

- Look at the sale and overstock pages on Web sites. Most retailers offer outlet, or sale, sections for their merchandise.

finding bargains on the web

Want the best price? These super sites scour the Internet for discounts, trusted retailers, and more.

SHOPZILLA.COM

- **Best for:** People who have a good idea of what they want— like your tween, say, who is begging for new pink sandals, without buckles, made by Skechers.
- **How this site helps:** It narrows down your choices. Search for an item, then choose a color, brand, and other details to eliminate unwanted options.
- **Standout feature:** Useful explanations. Buying a digital camera? Watch a video for expert advice.

SHOPPING.COM

- **Best for:** Shoppers who shop infrequently online.
- **How this site helps:** It has a clear, easy-to-read layout.
- **Keep your eye out for:** Smart Buy icons. These signal that the price shown is the lowest offered by a trusted merchant (a retailer with high consumer ratings). The site also features helpful buying guides.

PRICEGRABBER.COM

- **Best for:** Consumers who love to get a second opinion.
- **How this site helps:** It offers easy-to-access expert comments from the widest variety of sources. And you can participate in discussions with other shoppers.
- **Money savers:** Great coupons and rebates are just a click away. You can also request an e-mail alert to tell you when an item is available at the price you want to pay.

NEXTAG.COM

- **Best for:** Bargain hunters. Do you often wonder whether to give in and buy that camcorder or hold out in case it's $15 cheaper next week?
- **How this site helps:** It offers price histories, so you can see how much a product has been discounted recently. Like PriceGrabber, NexTag can send you an e-mail when an item has hit your preferred price.
- **Bonus:** Plenty of coupons and rebates are provided.

BEST OF THE WEB: general retailers

Try these sites for a broad range of merchandise.

Amazon (amazon.com). Sure, Amazon is great for books and music. But did you know that the site also stocks leather sofas, Kohler kitchen sinks, and  Weber grills—all for prices below those of most other retailers? Free shipping on most orders of $25 or more makes the bargains even better.

JCPenney (jcp.com). The site carries many items sold at its retail stores as well as products and sizes available only over the Web. Be sure to click on Outlet for discontinued and overstocked merchandise. Save on shipping when you have your order delivered to your nearest JCPenney rather than to your house. Need to send something back? You can return it to any of the stores or catalog desks for immediate credit.

Overstock (overstock.com). Be sure to check this site often. Overstocked items ranging from DVDs to living room furniture are available in limited quantities for a limited amount of time. If you can find what you want, you'll get rock-bottom prices.

web alert!

Shopping on the Web is a great way to get a fantastic bargain, but it also requires a few simple strategies to keep your money safe.

- Pay with your credit card. Your debit card doesn't protect you if the Web site you've used goes under; if you've used your credit card, you may get most or all of your money back.

- Shop at secure sites. Be sure to avoid sites that display a broken key or unlocked padlock at the bottom of your screen. These icons indicate that your transactions are not safe. Instead, look for the locked padlock as shown here.

- Install a secure browser. This will help foil hackers who try to gain access to your credit card information over the Web.

- Use security software that warns you when a site is not safe.

- Complicate your passwords. Choose passwords that others won't be able to figure out—don't use an address, phone number, or birthday—and change your password often. Use a blend of letters and numbers: If you choose a password that is a word in the dictionary, it's easy for hackers to figure it out.

- Alternate your passwords. If you write them down, keep them in a safe place.

- Print out your order. Keep a hard copy of all your orders in case something goes wrong.

do a google search for free repairs

Is something you own—a car or an appliance—on the fritz? You just might be able to save the cost of an expensive repair or replacement by searching on Google. A few smart mouse clicks can save you hundreds. Here are some tricks to try, with common examples.

- Cite the manufacturer in your search. Your Toyota Sienna's "check tire pressure" light keeps coming on. You can see that the tires are properly inflated, so the real problem is getting rid of the message. A mechanic could help, but instead, go to Google and type in "Toyota check tire pressure light." You'll get a link to material (not in the car manual) that explains how to temporarily disable the light. Savings: $100 for the dealer to diagnose the problem, plus the cost of any repair.

- Type in the error message. Your Epson printer has gotten huffy, flashing an "align print cartridges" message. The cartridges seem perfectly aligned, yet your printer isn't working. Turn to Google and type in "Epson align print cartridges." The responses include a link to a site with the you'd-never-figure-this-out solution (press two buttons at once to make the printer believe the faux problem is fixed.) Savings: $100-$200 (cost of a new printer).

- Be clear and concise. Your daughter's iPod appears to be dead. But before buying a new one, try to bring the old iPod back to life. Search on Google for "my iPod froze," and you'll be directed to werty.net, a blog that includes tech information (but also—fair warning—some four-letter words). The blog's two-step thawing trick: "Toggle the Hold switch on and off. (Slide it to Hold, then turn it off again.) Press and hold the Menu and Select (center button) buttons until the Apple logo appears, about 6 to 19 seconds." The iPod will revive. Savings: $249 (cost of a new iPod).

- Type in the brand and the word "problem." Your digital camera has stopped working. Go to Google again. Type in the brand plus "problem." A troubleshooting page explains that you likely have a defective memory card. Savings: about $265 (you'll spend $35 for a memory card instead of $300 for a camera).

- Specify that you need parts. Google can also help you locate repair parts for appliances. Let's say you need a new refrigerator-door bracket. Search for "GE replacement refrigerator parts" and you'll learn where to find the necessary model numbers. Install the $17 bracket yourself. Savings: $89.95, plus the cost of labor.

- Get good advice. Your son uses the Web when his VW Jetta gets cranky. He enters his problem at Google, then follows links to sites like bentleypublishers.com and vxvortex.com. There he finds posts from others on how they solved a similar problem.

wholesale clubs

Shopping at wholesale clubs is an adventure and can save you plenty of money, too. Just be sure to remember the following:

- Buy in bulk—but with a friend. Your family may not be able to polish off three dozen eggs that you buy at Costco before they expire, but you and a friend can split them— and the cost—and you'll both benefit. If you prefer shopping online, check out bythecase.net for places to buy all sorts of bulk items.

- Keep in mind that some warehouse clubs offer coupons to their members (even though they don't accept manufacturers' coupons).

- Here are the best deals on groceries at your discount warehouse: milk, spaghetti sauce, microwave popcorn, peanut butter, juice boxes, pickles, sugar-free sweeteners, and instant hot chocolate.

- And here are the best nonfood bargains: gas, brand-name clothing, film developing, baby wipes, Christmas decorations, laundry detergent, tires, and batteries.

dollar stores

Low operating costs and shelves filled with manufacturers' overstock items help keep prices low at dollar stores, especially on cleaning supplies and packaged goods.

- One recent example: Liquid Tide laundry detergent in the 100-ounce bottle was selling for $6.50 at Family Dollar, compared with $9.85 at a nearby grocery store. Chains like Dollar General (dollargeneral.com), Dollar Tree (dollartree.com), and Family Dollar (familydollar.com) are growing brands with thousands of stores across the country. (Log on to find a store near you.)

- Remember when you shop to pay attention to the quality of the product you're buying. A less expensive product won't save you money if it doesn't work or is defective.

store deals

Department stores, discounters, and other chain retailers are stepping up their promotions. Here's how you can benefit:

- Bloomingdale's, Lord & Taylor, and Macy's often send direct mail with coupons or alerts for upcoming sales. Other stores, such as Pottery Barn, e-mail regular customers about exclusive deals and special events.

- If you have a favorite store, ask for that store's credit card. You'll get discounts and coupons.

- Consider applying for a store's credit card when you're making a big purchase; you'll get a discount on the spot (usually 10 percent). Just check the interest rate before you sign up.

- Sometimes you don't have to wait in order to get a break. Before you buy an item, ask the clerk when it will go on sale. She may be able to tell you the date—or even make a deal on the spot.

- If you buy something only to notice it on sale a couple of days later, ask about a price adjustment. Big retailers such as Gap, Kohl's, and Target will refund the difference between what you paid and the discounted price. (There are restrictions; some retailers limit the adjustment to items purchased within the prior 14 days and that are accompanied by the original sales receipt.) Even stores without a formal price adjustment policy will sometimes honor the lower price—if you go back and ask.

yard sales

Yard sales benefit both sellers and buyers, particularly those who follow a few simple strategies. Here are tips for shoppers and sellers alike.

yard sale smarts for sellers

Yard sales and estate sales are wonderful places to find bargains and treasures; they can also work to your advantage when you want to sell your no-longer-needed stuff. Here are some money-making strategies:

- **Timing.** The best time to hold a yard sale is on a Sunday—many people reserve their Saturdays for errands, not yard sales—in May or September, since many potential shoppers go away in the summer. Start your sale as early as 7 A.M., so it will be the first stop for shoppers.

- **Publicity.** There are plenty of avenues for yard sale publicity:

   1. Distribute presale flyers featuring key items; post them on bulletin boards at grocery stores and other (approved) public places.

   2. Advertise on online classified sites—they're great for pulling in buyers from outside your area. Mention as many items as you can to attract collectors. Post two or three days before the sale, when serious shoppers map out routes. Ads may be free on craigslist.org and garagesalehunter.com; garagesalegal.com charges a small fee.

   3. Put an ad in your local paper, listing a few of your most interesting things and their prices.

- **Presentation.** Group your wares by category, since shoppers may come with particular needs, and stack clothes by size on tables. (Placing items on the ground forces customers to squat and discourages browsing.) Give bags to people clutching more than one item to free their hands for foraging.

From furniture to electronics, one person's trash is another's treasure—so when you want to dispose of an old item (and don't want to bother having a yard sale) don't make the dump your first stop. Two sites with alternatives: freecycle.org and earth911.org. The Freecycle Network describes itself as "a place to give or receive what you have and don't need or what you need and don't have—[to keep] stuff out of landfills." The Earth 911 Web site offers community-specific resources, with a focus on recycling. Check out the home page to find out where you can recycle your computer, your cell phone—even used motor oil.

- **Pricing.** There are a few strategies to consider about pricing:

   1. Charge in dollar increments to avoid making change—whether it's $1 per item or three or four pieces for $1. Small items that are priced to sell can really pull in the big bucks. It's psychological. Someone who won't pay $50 for a piece of furniture may think nothing of buying 15 items at $3 each.

   2. Yard sale shoppers often love to haggle, so let them. If you let them make an offer, they may be willing to pay even more than you would have suggested.

   3. When there's one hour left to closing, cut prices by 50 percent, but exempt items you can store until the next sale.

yard sale smarts for buyers

Just as yard sale sellers have strategies for selling (see above), yard sale shoppers have strategies for buying:

- Read presale flyers and ads for items you want, and ask if you can buy what you want—usually bigger items—before the sale even begins.

- Look for off-season items. For example, you might get a great deal on a Halloween costume in March, when the seller just wants to get rid of it.

- Arrive early. Try to shop right when the sale starts—before other shoppers have picked over the goods.

- Arrive late. Sellers may lower their prices simply so they don't have to keep all the items they were trying to sell.

- If the price is too high, make a reasonable offer. The worst the seller can say is no.

flea markets

Even more fun than yard sales, flea markets can be a bargain-hunter's paradise. Whether you're browsing for anything that catches your eye or searching for a particular piece for your living room, you need to keep these tips and strategies in mind.

- Get there early for the best selection. Dealers do, and so should you.

- Make a budget and stick to it. And remember, you have to love it to buy it.

- Negotiate. Sellers generally don't mind, as long as you do it respectfully. Ask for 15 to 20 percent off the marked price (with the item in your hands) on most items; ask for 10 percent on lower priced items (those under $10). If you're not comfortable negotiating with dollar amounts, you can always ask "Is this your best price?" or "Can you do better on this for me?" If you're interested in two pieces, you can ask for a price break if you take both. Finally, if you let the seller know you want a large item, ask for a break on a smaller item; she may even toss it into the deal for free.

- Pay in cash. More appealing to dealers than a check or credit card, cash is a potent bargaining chip.

- Bring up-to-date price guides with you. You'll be less likely to miss out on a bargain—or be taken.

- Make a low-ball offer if the item you want hasn't sold during the course of the flea market. The dealer may listen to your (reasonable) offer in order to bring in some cash.

- Protect yourself from fraud. Know how much the items you want to buy are worth (through books, trade publications, and online auctions), and ask for a receipt confirming that the item you bought is an original antique or collectible.

- Check dealers at the end of the day. You can find big bargains just before closing time and on the last day of the show. Dealers especially don't want to take home large items, simply to haul them to the next flea market, so you may be able to get a good price on furniture. The same holds true for seasonal shows, held two or three times a year—you'll probably get the best deal at the fall show, since dealers often use the winter as a time to restock.

- Look for quality, not quantity. If you're investing in items or if you plan to eventually sell your collection, buy quality items—those in the best condition or those with decorative or rare elements.

auctions

Auctions can save you lots of money—and be great fun in the process—or they can blow a huge hole in an overeager shopper's budget. Pay attention to the following strategies for online and traditional auctions to make sure you get some bang for your buck.

online auctions

Online auctions are all the rage, and you can find some wonderful items and even some fantastic prices on auction sites like eBay.com. But as with any financial transaction, there are certain rules you should follow in order to not get taken and to get the best price.

- Shop around before you bid. You may love the first item you see, but you'll probably love other items you see later even more.

- Don't rely on the photograph alone. Read the description of the item carefully to determine its exact size and condition. Photos can be deceiving.

- Research the seller of the item. Do they have a good rating in the Feedback section?

- Keep copies of all correspondence—whether by e-mail or snail mail—and transactions and records of conversations in case a dispute arises.

- Write down the top amount you're willing to spend on a particular item—and don't go above it. You don't want to overspend in the heat of the auction.

- Confirm the size, condition, and color of the item with the seller via e-mail through the auction site before you bid on it. Also, confirm the seller's refund policy and stated delivery schedule.

- Calculate the cost of postage into the cost of the item. Note that postage costs can vary on similar items from different sellers.

- Try to find sellers who use PayPal. It lets you pay without revealing your credit card information every time you shop, and it is a safe and easy way to make an online payment.

- Remember that you'll have to return the item at your own expense if you don't like what you've won.

traditional auctions

Traditional—meaning not online—auctions can save you a pretty penny. You still need to follow certain rules at old-fashioned auctions in order to protect yourself and get the best deal. Here's what you need to remember:

- Check out what's for sale at the preview, which usually takes place the week before the auction.

- Find out if taxes are owed on the item you want (a car or a boat, for example) and if they are, subtract that amount from your bid.

- Determine the payment policy. Does the auction require payment then and there? Does the auction accept personal checks?

- Look into the following types of auctions:

   1. U.S. Postal Service. You can find books, CDs, TVs, jewelry, and clothing at some postal auctions. Visit usps.com/auctions for more information. The postal service occasionally sells its damaged or undeliverable goods via eBay as well; visit pages.ebay.com/promo/usps.html to find out if an auction is happening.

   2. U.S. Department of the Treasury. The Treasury Department sells boats, jewelry, electronics, and other seized merchandise both online and in person (usually at the location of seized real estate). Visit ustreas.gov/auctions to see what's available.

3. U.S. Marshals Service. Even the U.S. Marshals have gotten into the auction act. Check out usdoj.gov/marshals to find out what bargains you can unearth from assets the Marshals have seized.

4. Federal, State, and Local Auctions. Visit usa.gov/shopping to view federal, state, and local auctions as well as auctions by federal agencies. You can search by state or even by type of seized asset.

BUYER BEWARE

Online auctions can put your money in jeopardy, so check out the following tips to keep your money safe:

Be on the alert for "positive feedback" scams. Some eBay operators compile high reliability ratings by selling inexpensive items—then skip out when unsuspecting buyers pay for pricier goods that never show up. To avoid getting fleeced, don't buy a costly item unless the seller has at least 1,000 comments (since a fishy seller won't invest the time to get such a large number). And look for consistency in the seller's merchandise. If he built up great ratings with $20 video games and is now selling $2,000 plasma TVs, be wary.

Put certain items on your "don't buy" list. Over the years, eBay has removed many inappropriate or unsafe offerings. But monitoring can't be perfect. So it's wise to steer clear of the following:

BUYER BEWARE

• **Makeup.** Used palettes, wands, and brushes are petri dishes for bacteria. A seller may claim her eyeliner is brand-new, but you can't be sure.

• **Designer bags.** The draw is obvious: getting a Chloé bag, say, for one-tenth its actual price. But it's a deal only if you're buying the real thing. Some are knock-offs, and you often can't tell whether the item has the necessary identifying labels or workmanship.

• **Cribs and bike helmets.** An older version may not be as safe as a newer one and may have been recalled. (Find recalled products at cpsc.gov.)

• **Laptops.** A secondhand model could have been dropped or banged around. With PCs now available for as low as $500 (and prices are still falling), why not just buy new?

• **DVD players.** A used model might seem to be in mint condition when you buy it, then die on you weeks later.

PART 2
GET A GOOD DEAL

Now that you know the essential shopping strategies, you can apply them when buying just about anything. And those strategies, combined with the information that follows, will help you get the best prices on whatever you have on your shopping list. Part 2 gives you money-saving tips on everything from curtains to pet food, from makeup to take-out, and from refrigerators to balmy resort vacations. Whether you choose to dip into the section most relevant to your shopping list or read the tips straight through, you'll find invaluable information that will slash your shopping costs.

contents

49

in and around the house

Keeping to a household budget can be a challenge. Everything from buying bed linens to heating your house—even buying food for your pet—adds up fast. Use the tips in this section to bring your costs down. (Be sure to check out the tips on buying household appliances on pages 100–109 as well.)

home decorating

From information on painting to vital money-saving tips for remodeling your bathroom, here is what you need to know to save on home decorating.

painting

- Paint is one of the least expensive decorating tools. Using color can help revitalize a living space, separate rooms, and set a mood. Buy several paint samples and try a few colors on the same wall, then look at the colors at different times of the day to see how they appear in natural light.

- Time is money, so when you're painting your house—either inside or out—be sure to paint in the fall, or whatever time of year you experience little rain and quiet weather. This will help you paint without interruption, and the paint will dry faster.

lighting

- Make the move to compact fluorescent light bulbs. They last longer than incandescent—up to ten times longer— and are four times more efficient. They cost more than ordinary incandescent bulbs, but you'll save on your electric bills in the long term. Use them in hallways, over front doors (if designated for outside), and other difficult bulb-changing places; you may not have to replace them for about six years.

PENNY WISE, POUND FOOLISH

You may think you're saving energy and money by turning off the lights for the split second you're out of a particular room, but don't turn them on and off constantly. Depending on your type of bulb, this on-again-off-again strategy can actually cost more—in terms of energy and bulb replacement—than just leaving the lights on. Incandescent bulbs, for example, should be turned off any time they're not needed, but compact fluorescent bulbs should be turned off only if you're leaving the room for more than 15 minutes.

LIGHT TOUCH

Lampshades are meant to hide ugly bulbs—so why aren't they always pretty themselves? You can inexpensively turn a humdrum cover into a custom stunner in mere minutes with some ribbon and fabric glue. Just affix ribbon around the edge of your shade and cut to fit. For a subtler accent, use a thin ribbon in a complementary hue; for a bold statement, go wide in a contrasting color. Guests will bask in your brilliance.

- To save more on lighting, install dimmer switches. Setting your dimmer at 75 percent output will save 20 percent in energy—and double the life of the bulbs.

- Use timers on your lights, indoors and out.

- Install motion sensors that work by turning lights on when you walk in, and off after no more motion is detected. Try them in entryways, hallways, garages, and near driveways. Don't install indoor sensors in high-traffic areas where they'll be continually triggered, and tweak outdoor sensors so they won't go on with every passing car. Look for outdoor detectors that are solar powered, meaning they charge during the day and don't draw off house electricity at all.

SCENTS FOR CENTS

Try these clever, inexpensive ways to add an appealing fragrance to any room in your house:

• **Maximize incense.** Place incense sticks in a vertical position for a slower, longer burn time.

• **Keep potpourri potent.** Refresh potpourri with this three-step process: Seal it in a plastic freezer bag with two or three drops of essential oil, shake it well, then let it sit for 24 hours in a closed cabinet. Repeat the process for even better results.

• **Reed diffusers** are an elegant way to spread aroma throughout a room, but their steep price—from $40 to $80 in many shops—can feel like a real stickup. Here's how to get the same sweet-smelling effect (and stylish look) without forking over so much cash: Fill a

small, clear glass vase or bottle with a bath oil that's powerfully fragrant (best bets include rose and lavender; some start as low as $5 for 10 ounces). Then snip off the ends of ordinary grill skewers and insert (flip them over whenever you want to refresh the intensity). Breathe in the scent of money well spent.

rugs

Area rugs come in a wide variety of sizes, colors, patterns—
and price. Use these strategies to find a rug to suit you and
your budget.

- Buy carpet remnants cheaply and have
  them bound and made into area rugs.

- If you change your décor nearly as
  often as you change your outfit, choose
  synthetic rugs—polypropylene or
  nylon—which provide water- and UV-
  resistance at low prices. A 5' x 8' can
  be had for less than $100. Nylon is the higher quality of
  the two because of its bulk (yarn made of polypropylene
  fibers can get crushed over time), plus it holds color well.
  But both synthetics are excellent at masking dirt.

PENNY WISE, POUND FOOLISH

Rug pads not only provide comfort and prevent slip-
ping, they can also add years to the life of the rug you
just purchased, since less movement means less fric-
tion (read: less wear and tear). So don't skip buying a
rug pad to save money. Most are made of synthetic
materials—such as PVC or latex—and though they vary
in thickness (a thicker one will make your rug feel
cushier), most have the same gripping capabilities. Buy
a pad that's one to two inches smaller than your rug,
and in your price range. (Pads range from $20 to $80.)

Company C (companyc.com). This site specializes in coordinated collections of rugs, pillows, and textiles. Click on a pillow, and you'll be shown, among other items, complementary draperies and sheets. For specials, click on Outlet, where discontinued items are often 50 percent off.

- Cotton rugs, $50 and up, are an even more affordable choice, but they can stain and wear out quickly (though you can throw them in a large washing machine).

- Want something eco-friendly? Plant-based fibers such as sisal, jute, and bamboo are not only biodegradable but made from renewable resources. Especially good for sunrooms or outdoor use because they shed water easily, plant-based fibers are difficult to clean and may last only a few years with heavy use; still, they start at a low $100.

- Remember that machine-made rugs generally cost less than a third of the price of hand-knotted versions.

furniture

- Look for sales on floor samples of furniture or simply ask if floor samples are available.

- Save 30 to 70 percent on previously leased furniture by shopping at rental centers. Check out clearance centers run by rental center chains like Cort Furniture Rental (cort.com) or regional rental centers.

- Make friends with the real estate agent who sells homes in new subdivisions. The agent will know when the furniture in the model homes will go on sale and may let you choose what you want before the sale. You'll get first crack at the furniture—and save big.

- Look for furniture showroom sales for discounts of 30 to 60 percent. You'll find furniture that's usually sold only to professional designers. You can gener-ally find showrooms in cities like Chicago (Chicago's Merchandise Mart, mmart.com/designcenter/), Seattle (The Seattle Design Center, seattledesigncenter.com), and Los Angeles (L.A. Mart, mmart.com/lamart/designcenter/).

- Check out government auctions of seized or abandoned fur-niture (and other items) at government-auctions-guide.com. You can also search for auction lists for free on sites like usa.gov. Visit your local government's Web site to see if they sell or give away furniture.

- Office furniture and office supply stores— and their corresponding Web sites— occasionally have sales on furniture. Try sites like furniturefinders.com and Used Office Furniture Depot (used-office-furniture-depot.com).

- Don't forget to bargain. Big furniture pieces—like couches and dining-room tables—are usually marked up by 100 percent or more, so furniture salespeople have lots of room to negotiate on the price.

- Do your homework before you shop. Find out what discounters and auction- or comparison-shopping Web sites like mysimon.com, nextag.com, and ebay.com are asking for the item you want; then ask your local store to match the lowest price. Be sure to find out the tax and delivery charges.

- Time your shopping expedition so you arrive at the furniture store when it's pretty empty. Sales reps will be eager to make a sale and therefore be more likely to negotiate.

- Buy quality furniture that will last. It will be less expensive in the long run.

- As with clothing, accessories, and appliances, ask for a discount if the furniture you want has a scratch or other small imperfection.

- Ask for a break on the price if your furniture has been slightly damaged on delivery. Call the store manager and nicely offer to keep the item in exchange for a discount; a $25 or $50 price break will be more palatable to the manager than having to pick up the damaged piece of furniture and deliver the second one.

- Don't be afraid to ask for a discount, even after you've bought the furniture. If you find a better deal at a competitor before your furniture is delivered, call the store where you bought the item to cancel delivery; the salesperson may offer to match the lower price.

- Check out estate sales, yard sales, and even stores that buy furniture from estate sales for deals.

- Look online for free furniture. Craigslist.org and freecycle.com are good starting points.

HOW TO NEGOTIATE

You: Is this your best price for this armoire?

Them: The price is marked.

You: Wasn't this recently on sale? Do you think you could honor that recent sale price? I could wait for your next sale, but I'm sure I'll find this cheaper somewhere else in the meantime.

Pottery Barn (potterybarn.com). If you're looking to order big pieces of furniture sight unseen, Pottery Barn delivers consistent quality with dependable service. Plus, you'll find links to Pottery Barn Kids and PB Teen. Best feature: Customer service. A representative will e-mail you updates if your item is back-ordered and resolve problems if something is damaged during delivery.

Ballard Designs (ballarddesigns.com). Selection is this site's strong point. You'll find quality furniture and accessories for every room in a wide range of prices. Best feature: Want to see that armchair in a different fabric? Click on the solid, plaid, or print of your choice, and the picture of the chair will update on your screen.

window treatments

- Make your own kitchen curtains in minutes, sans needle and thread. Start with two pretty, oversized dishtowels. Slide clip rings onto a rod. Clip the towels on and you're in business. It sure beats the prices of curtains at your local linens store. The rods and rings are available from the Antique Drapery Rod Co. (antiquedraperyrod.com).

- If you're handy with a needle and thread, you can save a bundle on bedroom curtains. Purchase king-size flat sheets in the same pattern as your bed linens, and sew yourself custom, designer window treatments.

- Use a twin sheet rather than an expensive liner to line homemade curtains.

- Not a big fan of sewing? You can still save money hemming curtains yourself by using Stitch Witchery. Simply use this iron-on hemming tape and your curtains will look custom made.

- If you like a custom roller shade but don't like the expense, buy a no-sew fabric roller shade kit. It lets you cut shades to your window specs; best of all, you can iron fabric onto the shades to match your décor.

- Simple roller shades are inexpensive and come in hundreds of fabrics, colors, textures, and prints. These high-end looking window treatments are a comparatively priced alternative to plain white roller shades.

- Simple cotton or linen panels are reasonably priced and never go out of style. When decorating trends change, your curtains will stay the same.

- Remember that white curtains match any décor. You can take them when you move, avoiding the expense of buying new curtains.

- Tension rods for café curtains have been upgraded. They're now handsome—and still affordable—and will add pizzazz to any window treatment.

BEST OF THE WEB: window treatments

Budget Blinds (budgetblinds.com). Buy inexpensive window treatments—from woven wood blinds to cellular shades—at this helpful Web site. It offers a wide selection of name brands, free in-house consultation, and expert measuring and installation—all at an affordable price.

Pearl River (pearlriver.com). Known for its exquisite, quality Chinese goods, Pearl River offers bamboo blinds, paper blinds, plantation blinds, and fabric blinds. These window treatments give you a high-end look at a fraction of the cost.

Great Windows (greatwindows.com). Ordering window treatments online is a challenge. Measure incorrectly, and you're likely to get stuck with something that doesn't fit anywhere. But Great Windows posts excellent instructions for measuring, ordering, and installing. Best features: The firm will send out up to five swatches for free, and products come with a 100-year warranty.

- Temporary curtains don't have to temporarily bankrupt you. If you're waiting for window treatments, cover your windows with inexpensive paper accordion blinds (cut to fit your window) from your home store retailer.

- Look for a community curtain exchange. See if there's a window treatment consignment shop near you.

- If your bathroom window doesn't have frosted glass and you don't want to block the light with curtains, buy adhesive window film. The film makes your window look frosted, so you get privacy without losing the light—all for a great price.

- Drapery hardware can cost a small fortune. But that doesn't mean you have to settle for boring, budget models. One stylish alternative that won't break the bank: a length of bamboo. At a garden supply store, choose a piece in its light natural hue, or a pre-stained version. Measure your window's width and saw the piece to fit (it's easiest if you secure the rod with a bench vise or a clamp). For a more polished look, hot-glue a coordinating button to each end. Then mount the new pole as you would any curtain rod—and pat yourself on the back for getting the goods while beating the price.

bedding

BED LINENS

- Don't just dream about reducing the cost of pillowcases. If you can sew, you can make three pillowcases out of a twin-size flat sheet for less than half the cost of a set of two.

- Make your own comforter covers and save a bundle. Take two sheets, sew three sides together, then add some type of closure (Velcro, for example) to secure the fourth side.

- Don't spend a lot for an overly high thread count—200–500 will feel perfectly silky. (Kids' sheets are usually 180.) The type of cotton used is more important than the thread count. Egyptian, Supima, and Pima are good quality and will last.

- Buy plain-style sheets for savings. Hem stitching, piping, and eyelet trim will add to the cost of your sheets.

- Wait for a traditional white sale in January and August for sheets and comforters. In fact, some retailers are putting bed linens on sale throughout the year, so you should never pay full price for them.

- Use a mattress pad, even if you have a mattress topper (which can't be cleaned) with a cover. A mattress pad will protect your mattress and make it last longer. Use a waterproof mattress pad for children's beds.

BEST OF THE WEB: bedding

Down Home Outlet (downhomeoutlet.com). The focus here is on sheets, pillows, and comforters. Best feature: Every product comes with a three-year guarantee; standard shipping is free.

- Pillows can be tough to buy, since you never know if you'll be happy with them when you get them home. Check the store's return policy. You may have 30 days to return the pillow if it doesn't feel right to you.

- Know how you sleep (on your stomach, side, or back) before buying a pillow. Many pillows are designed for specific sleep positions.

MATTRESSES

- Never pay full price for a mattress. In fact, you can get up to 20 percent off the price listed at the showroom or quoted over the phone (through 1-800-Mattress, for example) if you just ask. If you spend more than $500, you should get a free frame and free delivery with your mattress. If the retailer doesn't offer those, ask for a bigger discount.

- Don't waste your money on pillow-top padding. Though the extra cushion sewn on top of the mattress looks inviting, it easily adds $100 to the cost of the mattress—and has been known to flatten or sag as the mattress ages.

- Don't forget the hidden cost of new sheets when you buy a new mattress. And beware of sheets advertised as "guaranteed to fit all"—they usually fit mattresses that are actually 15 inches deep at the most, and today's mattresses can be as thick as 20 inches. If your mattress is more than 15 inches thick, buy sheets with extra-deep corners or pockets.

BUYER BEWARE

Never buy a used mattress, no matter the price. You can't know what quality you're getting.

remodeling
GENERAL TIPS

- Whether you're redoing your bathroom, kitchen, or basement, try to schedule your remodeling job for the winter. Contractors are generally less busy during the colder months, which is good news for you: the job will be finished faster and could cost less than in summer.

- Want a remodeling project that will almost pay for itself? Kitchens and bathrooms are your best bet, as are most kinds of landscaping and side paneling. Check with your local real estate agent and appraiser to find out which projects add the most value in your neighborhood.

- Don't go overboard. Buyers looking for a nice house in an average neighborhood may not pay for fancy improvements like granite countertops and designer faucets.

- Make sure your remodeling project doesn't turn your house into the fanciest one on the street. You may not recoup your remodeling costs.

- Purchase energy-efficient kitchen appliances and double-pane windows and you'll recover some of your remodeling costs (through reduced energy bills) even before you sell your home.

- Be careful about cutting costs on remodeling. For example, if you install a deck that's too small, your house may lose value when it comes time to sell.

- Improve your outdoor space to add value to your home. You can recoup your cost of improvement by creating a patio made of clay or concrete pavers. They come in a wide range of shapes and colors, are easy to install, and cost less than a wooden deck. If you decide instead to make a deck, be sure to use low-maintenance materials.

- Add an accent light under a pretty tree or install solar lights along a walk to make a big change in how your house looks for very little investment.

- Don't add a pool to your house in order to add value to your property. It's a big expense that rarely pays off when you sell your home.

- Carefully plan your remodeling job. If you don't, you may substantially increase the cost of the project with hidden expenses that start to crop up.

- Need tools for your remodeling job? Savvy manufacturers of cordless tools offer cordless tool kits at substantial savings over buying the tools individually. The money-saving secret is that all of the tools in the kit use the same battery. Since the battery is one of the most expensive parts of a cordless tool, you save big by not having to pay for multiple batteries. Cordless kits vary in size; among others you can find a two-tool kit consisting of a drill and a flashlight as well as a five-tool kit offering a drill, trim saw, jig saw, power planer, and flashlight.

THE KITCHEN

- What do home buyers look for in a kitchen? Wooden cabinets, work islands, ceramic tile floors, solid-surface and granite countertops, and energy-saving new appliances. Anything you can do to make your kitchen

THE WHEEL DEAL

Want attention-getting kitchen hardware? Skip the overpriced brass pulls, and try this plumb genius idea instead:

Repurpose bright-red sillcock wheel handles, or hose-cock handles, used on outdoor faucets, to get an instant splash of color and conversation-starting shape. (To mount, you'll need a bolt that fits through the handle and a rod coupling that fits the bolt.) The price is right—a few bucks.

homier, more open, or more useful will pay you back when you sell your house.

- You can give your kitchen a quick face-lift without spending your life's savings. Simply scrub your cabinets with a degreaser to lighten the look of the whole room.

- If new cabinets aren't in the cards, try refacing your old cabinets. It's cheaper and looks great.

- If refacing isn't enough, you still don't have to replace your cabinets in their entirety. Just replace the cabinet doors.

- Spruce up your cabinets with new drawer pulls. A simple change from plain old knobs to new ceramic (or even leather) hardware can immediately and inexpensively transform the look of your kitchen.

- For a low-cost alternative to kitchen hanging bars, look to bath accessories. Basic towel racks with simple S hooks can serve as hanging racks in the kitchen. Short towel racks attached on the inside of cabinet doors can be used as lid holders.

- Is your refrigerator looking worn but working perfectly well? Don't rush out to buy a new one; simply spruce up your old one with appliance epoxy paint. Check out Rust-Oleum's appliance epoxy in Stainless Steel.

- Don't forget that new faucets can work wonders in the kitchen. This minor investment will have a major impact.

- Many home-store chains offer free computer-aided kitchen design and knowledgeable consultants. Take advantage of these services.

- You can make small, inexpensive improvements in a bathroom that will have a big impact. Simply adding new sink faucets can change the entire look of the room.

- Another small change: if you have a small bathroom, replace a hulking vanity sink with a streamlined pedestal sink. (This could be a big job, though, depending on your plumbing.)

- Nothing dates a bathroom faster than a pastel-pink tub. Stick to timeless hues for pricey purchases, then make a splash with inexpensive accents like candles and vases.

- Cheaper than replacing the vanity, new lighting can give a face-lift to the entire bathroom.

SAVING $ SAVES THE ENVIRONMENT

Buy water-efficient showerheads. With low-flow models, a family of four can cut water usage by as much as 280 gallons a month—and yet not feel much difference in water pressure.

GET MORE FOR LESS

Improve the curb appeal of your house and you may be able to sell it faster, and for more than if it didn't call out to prospective buyers. Here are inexpensive fixes you can make for dramatic results:

Repaint or touch up the paint on the outside of your house.

Clean your windows. Your house will look better inside and out.

Trim shrubs so they stay below windowsills.

Give or throw away lawn clutter like broken lawn furniture and old, unused swing sets.

Add color to patios and front porches with bright flowers in outdoor planters. (You can take the planters with you when you move.)

BEST OF THE WEB: hardware and more

Van Dykes Restorers (vandykes.com). Renovating? This site has vintage hardware, doorknobs, cabinet pulls, and glass chandelier pendants. Items like solid brass hinges and drawer pulls have sold for as little as $1.99 each.

cleaning

Surprisingly, you can save money while doing everyday chores, like cleaning. Here are helpful money-saving tips from dusting to carpet-cleaning to full-blown spring cleaning, as well as for dishes and the laundry.

cleaning around the house

- Spring-clean in the fall? You bet. Save time and money by spring-cleaning at the most logical time of year—fall. Open windows in summertime bring in the dirt, so rather than spending money to clean in the spring and watch the dirt accumulate in the summer, do your heavy-duty cleaning in the fall. You'll get the added advantage of having a shimmering house for the holidays.

- Ask for the whole-house rate when inquiring about the cost of cleaning your carpets. You'll probably get a discount over cleaning a series of individual rooms.

- Pour 1 quart of boiling water mixed with ¼ cup ammonia into your drains monthly to minimize or eliminate clogs.

- Make your own dust cloths from old flannel pajamas, an old flannel sheet, or discarded T-shirts. Simply clean the homemade cloths in the washing machine and reuse. Don't use sections of fabric with seams, buttons, or other rough areas that can scratch furniture.

- Save money on cleaning products—and save lots of time in the process—by quickly wiping the cabinets nearest your stove with a damp cloth every few days to keep grease and soil from building up.

- If you're having your windows professionally cleaned, save on prep fees by removing draperies and blinds ahead of time and clearing any furniture that could obstruct the workers' access.

SAVING $ SAVES THE ENVIRONMENT

Make your own cleaning products and save:

Brass and Copper Cleaner Dissolve 1 teaspoon of salt in 1 cup of white vinegar. Add enough flour to make a paste. Apply the paste; let stand for 15 minutes. Rinse with clean, warm water; towel dry.

Window Cleaner Mix 2 tablespoons of clear ammonia with 1 quart of water.

All-purpose Scouring Cleanser Use baking soda on a damp sponge or cloth to clean stains, scuffs, and surfaces all around the house.

dishes

• The rinse-and-hold cycle on your dishwasher is more efficient than your sink to rinse only a few dishes.

• Powders, liquids, and packets can all clean well. But the detergent has to be fresh or it won't do the job. A good rule of thumb: buy only what you can use within two months. And you should always store it in a cool, dry spot—not under the sink, where detergent can clump or deteriorate.

• Use only detergents designed for use in automatic dishwashers. Do not put detergent in the dispenser(s) until it is time to run the dishwasher; it can cake and fail to dissolve—wasting both your time and your money.

- Compare the costs of different forms of detergent. Single dose packets, while convenient, can cost more per use than powder.

laundry

- Cut down the use of hot water in the wash. Use warm water, and you'll cut your energy use.

- Use powder laundry detergent. It's great at getting out ground-in dirt and often costs less per use than liquid detergent.

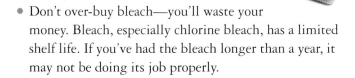

- Don't over-buy bleach—you'll waste your money. Bleach, especially chlorine bleach, has a limited shelf life. If you've had the bleach longer than a year, it may not be doing its job properly.

- Treating stains promptly not only increases the rate of success of removing stains but also saves you time and money. Your dry-cleaning bills will diminish, and your clothing will last longer.

- Although many people swear by club soda as a stain remover, there seems to be no scientific basis for its popularity. The fact that it is generally right at hand, so that the stain is treated promptly, probably accounts for its success. Plain tap water is cheaper and works just as well.

- In-home dry-cleaning kits are an economical solution for removing odors and stains from dry-clean-only items. They work particularly well on sweaters and items with beads, sequins, and other special-care trims and can extend the time between dry cleanings. Follow the clothing's label instructions and check for colorfastness before using the stain-removal system that comes with these kits. (For heavily soiled or stained items, a professional dry cleaner is a better solution.) You can save about $200 per year simply by cleaning one suit every other week with a dry-cleaning kit, rather than taking it to a dry-cleaner.

how your house works

You may not think you can save money on the inner workings of your house, but you'd be surprised by the amount you can save on these features of your home. Try the following tips to save big.

heating

- Lower your thermostat. Dial down by two degrees and you could save about $40 on your heating bills.

- Install a programmable thermostat. Save as much as $100 a year by letting your thermostat lower the heat 10 to 15 percent when you're asleep or at work.

- Turn down your water heater. Lower your energy costs by 3 to 5 percent by reducing the water temperature by only ten degrees. How low should you go? You can have a nice, steamy shower at 120 degrees.

- Lower your curtains and shades. Leaky windows can cost you up to 25 percent of the energy used to heat and cool your home. Use cellular window shades, which feature air pockets that help keep the heat in your house. You can save even more by using twill curtains with foam bonded onto the fabric or heavy, lined drapes.

- Use a space heater if you spend much of your time in only one room of your home, while keeping the overall house temperature lower. If you keep the thermostat at 62 degrees and put a space heater in one room, you can save about $200 a year. (Be sure to place the space heater on a hard and level surface, three feet or more from anything flammable or that could block air intake or heat output. Read all the warnings that come with the product, and, of course, keep children and pets away.)

- Buy an energy-efficient furnace and water heater. Always look for the Energy Star label when replacing a furnace or water heater; it will help you save up to 20 percent on your energy bill. Keep in mind that technological improvements can help you save on appliances as well. If you're in the market for a new water heater, for example, try a tankless water heater, which warms up cold water quickly when it's needed, without wasting energy. This appliance could save you 25 to 45 percent on your water-heating costs.

- Plant trees. Add deciduous trees to the south and west sides of your house. The leaves will help keep your house cool in the summer, and the sun will still warm your house in the winter, after the leaves have fallen. You can save up to $250 a year if you plant three trees in the right spots.

WARMTH WITHOUT HEAT

Stay warm in the winter without adding to your heating costs by adopting the following easy solutions.

• **Wear slippers.** Your mother always said that heat escapes through your head and your feet, and she was right. Try wool, felt, shearling, or faux-shearling slippers to keep your feet—and consequently the rest of your body—warm on cold days and nights. Ankle-high down booties work well, too.

• **Choose the right bedding.** If you really want to be warm at night, use flannel sheets, a Polarfleece blanket, and a down comforter on your bed. You'll be even warmer if you wear Polarfleece or flannel pajamas and socks. With the right blankets and the right bed clothes, you can turn the heat down to 58 degrees at night and save about $100 over the course of the winter.

• **Enjoy some soup.** Don't forget that your insides have to be warm, too! Use the smallest pot and the smallest burner possible for heating up the soup (to save energy). Copper-bottom cookware is your best bet for heating up your soup fast.

• **Wear a sweater.** Layer up to keep warm rather than raise the thermostat. Polarfleece will keep you warm, but an even better bet is a sweater made out of wool, cashmere, or mohair.

- Have your furnace inspected once a year for cleaner air and greater efficiency. After it has been inspected, vacuum the exterior. During the heating season, clean all vents, baseboards, or radiators once a month to keep your system in tip-top shape—and to save on heating costs.

- Wrap your water heater in an insulation blanket. You'll lower the cost of running it by up to 9 percent.

- To prevent freezing, insulate any pipes running through the unheated areas of your house with lengths of closed-cell foam tubes. These are split to slip easily over the pipes. Insulation also stops "sweating" in hot weather, and in time pays for itself by saving energy.

- Add insulation any time you make a renovation. You'll recoup your costs in heating bills over time.

- Ask your electric/gas company for an energy audit, often free. Your carrier can check seals around doors and windows and inspect appliances, and let you know where you need to make changes in order to save on utility bills.

- Replace old, cracked, or missing weather stripping around exterior doors.

- Improve the seal of interior doors (like the one to the garage) by attaching a sweep. Sold at hardware stores, these flexible plastic strips are easily screwed to door bottoms and keep out cold air from below.

- Make a preemptive strike against high bills by taking a caulk gun to cracks and gaps in your house and save hundreds in the process.

   1. Look carefully at your windows and doors, particularly at cracks in the panels or gaps behind the frames. Check both interiors and exteriors. Stand outside and shine a flashlight on your doors and windows; if your helper on the inside can see the light though cracks and gaps, you need to seal them.

   2. You need two tools to seal your home: caulk and a caulk gun. Latex caulk works well on inside areas because it can be painted, while silicone is better for outside areas because it's mildew-resistant and will expand and contract with temperature fluctuations. When you're shopping for a caulk gun, make sure it feels comfortable to grip and unlikely to jam. (You can also use a squeeze tube of caulk—which doesn't require a gun—if you're not planning to use a lot.)

   3. Clean the area you're working on with soap and water (use rubbing alcohol for tough spots), then chip off old paint and caulk with a putty knife and a razor blade. Cut the tip of the caulk tube on a diagonal and then load the gun. You may want to practice drawing a few lines on a piece of cardboard before you start. After that, you're ready to start caulking—and saving on your heating bills.

- Seal indoor leaks to save energy dollars. Draft leaks are often found behind electrical outlets and light switches. You can seal them with expanding foam, which comes in a spray can. Here's how:

    1. Turn off the power to the receptacle or switch. Remove the cover plate and the receptacle or switch.

    2. Squirt the expanding foam in any gaps between the electrical box and the surrounding wall covering, wearing disposable gloves. (Do not squirt the foam inside the box itself.) Important: apply in small amounts, because the foam generally expands to two to three times its original size.

    3. Let the foam dry; remove any excess with a sharp utility knife.

    4. Replace the parts and turn on the current.

cooling

- Be sure to wipe the outside of all your room air conditioners—especially the vents—every year to make them work more effectively (and use less electricity).

- Clean the filter monthly during the summer. How? Remove the filter, vacuum it, and then rinse it under running water. You can also use a toothbrush to clean it.

- Little changes mean big savings when using an air conditioner. Set the thermostat for a comfortable 78 (or use the "low" setting on most window units). Just three degrees lower and you'll pay about 18 percent more; about five degrees lower will cost you 39 percent more.

- Unplug your air conditioners in the off-season so they won't draw current and you'll save on your electric bill.

- Install the central air conditioner's condenser on the north side of your home, out of direct sunlight.

- Install awnings over windows not shaded by a roof overhang.

- Draw draperies and blinds during hot days.

- Minimize use of heat-generating appliances, such as the range, during hot weather. Use appliances in morning or at night—not during middle of the day—if you have to use them at all.

- Take advantage of cool summer days. Open windows and turn off the air conditioner.

- Make sure your cooling system has a SEER (Seasonal Energy Efficiency Ratio) or EER (Energy Efficiency Ratio) rating above 9. The minimum SEER rating for new systems is 13.

- Use window fans and ceiling fans instead of air conditioners. A window fan can create a pleasant breeze using about one tenth of the electricity an air conditioner needs.

- Use your attic fan to cool the whole house in the summer. Just be sure to cover it in the winter so cold air from the attic doesn't cool you down in the wrong season!

plumbing

- A running toilet will cost you plenty in wasted water, high water bills, and a plumber's time and labor. You can avoid all this by taking the following simple steps.

  1. Lift off the tank's lid and take a look. If water is overflowing into the vertical tube, you'll need to lower the water level in the tank. To do so, simply bend the arm on the float downward, or, in newer models, squeeze the adjustment clips and slide the float down.

  2. If the water level isn't the problem, add a little food coloring to the tank and wait about 20 minutes. A change in color in the toilet bowl means the flapper—a rubber diaphragm at the bottom of the tank—is leaking and needs to be replaced. Turn off the water supply behind the toilet and pop out the flapper with your hands. Take it to a hardware store and ask for a replacement. The new one should pop back in the same way.

- Stop dripping faucets. Though it's hard to believe, those drops will cost you in your water bill.

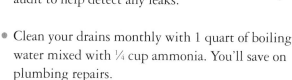

- Ask your water company for a free water use audit to help detect any leaks.

- Clean your drains monthly with 1 quart of boiling water mixed with ¼ cup ammonia. You'll save on plumbing repairs.

roofing

- Raise the roof with recycled materials! If your old shingles need replacing, consider a Classic Metal Roofing System (classicroof.com). It's made from up to 95 percent recycled aluminum but resembles traditional shakes or tiles. It's 100 percent recyclable if it ever has to be replaced, and it may qualify you for a tax credit.

gardening

Nothing spruces up a house's presentation like a well-tended lawn and blossoming trees and flowers. Here are ways to cut costs while you grow your garden.

flowers, trees, and shrubs

- Wait until the end of the summer season to landscape. You can find deals on the plants, trees, and shrubs you want.

- Get inexpensive trees while you help the environment. Become a member of the National Arbor Day Foundation for $10 and receive ten free trees in return. Visit arborday.org for details.

- Plant fresh seeds. Check for freshness by placing about 20 seeds on a damp towel or paper towel for a week; about 60 to 70 percent should start to sprout. If your seed test gives you a smaller crop, toss them and buy more—or you'll have to resow, which will cost you money.

- Make sure the soil pH is suitable before you plant. Your local garden center or county-run horticultural center may pH test a soil sample for you for free, or you can buy an inexpensive pH test kit at a garden center or hardware store.

GET MORE FOR LESS

Container gardening is an inexpensive way to brighten up any patio or porch. Use old buckets or wooden boxes—even an old bathtub will work—filled with flowers to add spots of color around your house. As long as your container has drainage holes, you don't need to spend money on new containers.

- Buy small- to medium-size plants with good color and noticeable growth when planning your vegetable garden. Larger plants may not take as well to transplantation; their roots, which have been balled up in a small container, may become stressed as they stretch out.

- Sanitize your tools throughout the season so they don't spread plant disease throughout the garden. Dip them in either boiling water or 70 percent rubbing alcohol.

- Be sure to place your plants far enough apart so that they can grow—and so they won't spread disease. Get instructions on proper spacing from the seed packet or your local nursery.

garden decorations

- What gardener hasn't lingered over the gorgeous cedar potting benches on display in stores? But at $400 and up, perfection is pricey. Here's an attractive, thrifty version, for a garage or basement, that will round up your tools and give you a good workspace—for less than $100. Mount a section of lattice on a wall; center two adjustable sawhorses in front, and lay a precut Formica counter on top (all available at your local home store).

- Don't overpay for cutesy or clunky storage bins. Media and desk accessories are sleek and inexpensive, so try repurposing a CD box (for corralling bulbs) or a wire shelf (to keep pots off your work area). Attach to the lattice, if you have it, with hooks or brackets.

BEST OF THE WEB: gardening

Gurney's Seed & Nursery (gurneys.com). This site is great for vegetable and flower seeds, trees, shrubs, bulbs, and plants. Best feature: The "Hardiness Grow Zone" map tells you which kinds of plants will grow in your zip code.

Gardener's Supply Company (gardeners.com). Get all the tools you need to make your garden grow. Great deal: Click on Outlet for big savings.

- To add country charm on the cheap, shop for simple sec-ondhand pieces at flea markets that can spruce up any garden. An old-fashioned wall sconce can be reborn as an outdoor candlestick, for example—just replace the glass with a simple pillar candle.

- If metal chairs are rusty but worth restoring, do the trick with a bright-white spray-on enamel.

the lawn

- Reseed your lawn at the right time of year—from Labor Day to Columbus Day—to avoid paying for grass seed that doesn't sprout. Grass seed is more likely to grow in the fall, when weeds like crabgrass have died off. Root systems will absorb fertilizer better then, too.

- Mow your grass yourself. You'll save the cost of a lawn service and get good exercise in the process.

pets

Just like people, pets need good food, high-quality health care—even insurance. Here are tips to help keep pet costs down.

health

- Never skip your pet's health-care appointments in order to save money—preventative veterinary care will save you more money than it will cost you over the long run.

- Pay one price for many pets at the vet. Take the family dog, your child's hamster, and any other pets in the house to the vet on the same day for their annual checkup. Your vet may charge you per visit, rather than per animal.

- Ask your vet if she offers senior pet discounts.

- Get long-term vaccines when possible. Your pet may not need an annual rabies shot; some vets offer rabies vaccines that last three years, rather than one. The vet may offer long-term booster shots, too.

- Spay or neuter your pet. It will save you the cost of future health care—it reduces the risk of breast, ovarian, and uterine cancer in females and testicular cancer in males— and the cost of a surprise litter.

- Ask for a second opinion. If your vet recommends expensive surgery or diagnostic imaging, get another vet to concur before forking over your paycheck.

- Think outside the vet box. Take your pet to a vet school or a humane society or shelter that offers basic health care for less than the vet. Your local department of health is a good resource too; they may offer rabies shots for significantly less than you're used to paying. Visit pets911.com to find a clinic in your neighborhood that you can use.

- Do weekly check-ups at home to avoid more costly problems later. According to the ASPCA, you should do the following every week:

    1. Check for lumps, bumps, flakes, or scabs under your pet's fur.

    2. Look for redness or discharge in your pet's eyes and his ears.

    3. Make sure your pet's eating and drinking habits have not changed. If they have, call the vet immediately.

    4. Clean your pet's ears.

    5. Brush your pet's teeth with a pet toothbrush and pet toothpaste and make sure his gums look healthy.

    6. Smell your pet's breath. Digestive problems can show up as bad breath.

- Consider adopting your pet from an animal shelter, where they may offer free vaccinations and neutering or spaying.

- As with any health care, keep detailed records of your pet's shots and treatments for future vet appointments. You'll save time and money if you know what care your pet has already received.

SUPER SITES FOR PET OWNERS

Search online for *pet care* and you'll be handed 195 million links (yes, really), with no way to evaluate them. So don't waste time sifting. These two sites offer a combination of low prices and good advice, and they're both vet recommended.

petsmart.com Find everything from cat scratching posts to a Pink Princess Hamster Castle. Bonus feature: Dozens of articles on pet health, behavior, training, and more. Does your dog bite? Find out how to curb the bad habit.

drsfostersmith.com Buy vet-selected supplies at a discount. Plus, get good information on grooming and other topics. Bonus feature: An online pharmacy. (See page 94 for more information on pet medicine.)

pet medicine

- According to some TV ads, you'll get the best prices on pet pills by calling a discount seller toll free—but once you've paid the shipping, are you really getting a deal? To find out, *Good Housekeeping* asked vets nationwide what they charge for a set of common meds (two prescribed, two over-the-counter), then compared those prices with what *Good Housekeeping* was charged (including shipping costs) by popular discounters, and found that the discounters often saved customers a bundle. These discounters include Doctors Foster and Smith (drsfostersmith.com), VetAmerica (vetamerica.com), PetMed Express (1800petmeds.com), and PetCareRx (petcarerx.com).

food

- Buy pet food at a pet discounter where prices are significantly lower than at the vet and you can buy in bulk, saving even more.

- The ASPCA recommends buying premium-quality dog or cat food because cheaper foods may contain filler material that doesn't include nutrients and can aggravate allergies and digestive problems.

- Don't overfeed your pet. Overfeeding leads to higher food costs and higher vet costs due to problems that are associated with obesity.

- Take advantage of rewards programs at pet stores. With Petco's P.A.L.S. program, for instance, you'll earn a free bag of premium cat or dog food when you purchase ten bags within 12 months.

grooming

- Regularly brush your pet. You won't have to pay a groomer and you'll have less hair in your house. Cats will experience fewer hairballs as well.

- Cut your pet's nails yourself, and do it on a regular basis. Again, you'll save the cost of a groomer and probably the cost of replacing scratched furniture and torn curtains.

toys

- Pets—like children—are happy with simple toys. Forgo the expensive pet-shop toys and give your dog a tennis ball. He'll be just as happy.

- Rotate your pets' toys. They'll be delighted when you reintroduce a toy, and you won't have to buy new toys nearly as often.

BEST OF THE WEB: pet goods

Check out purina.com, where you'll find lots of money-saving coupons for dog food, cat litter, and so on.

insurance

- Just like people, pets get sick. And health care costs for pets, as well as people, can be high. Now you can buy insurance for your pet, just as you do for yourself. But should you spring for it? That depends on a number of factors.

Buy it if:

1 You have a puppy or kitten, since these babies are more likely to have accidents.

2 Money is tight. Insurance makes sense particularly in the first year of your pet's life, since a wellness plan (for about $18 a month) will cover most shots and exams.

3 You will do anything to keep your pet alive. Modern medicine can save pets that in the past would have been euthanized, but you'll pay a lot for it.

4 You have an outside pet. Outdoor animals are more susceptible to illness and injury than indoor pets.

5 Your pet comes from a shelter. You can get a short-term policy that will cover problems like viruses or kennel cough brought home from the shelter.

Don't buy it if:

1 Your pet is no longer a youngster. The cost of insurance doubles as the pet gets older.

2 Your pet is susceptible to genetic problems due to his breed. Many insurance plans won't cover hereditary illnesses or cover them only for a large fee.

3 Your pet has a preexisting medical condition.

4 The pet insurance company isn't licensed. You won't recoup your costs if the company declares bankruptcy. (However, you'll be covered if the insurer is licensed in your state and is underwritten by another carrier.)

big-ticket items

Whether you're buying groceries that will disappear in a week or looking for a refrigerator that will last years, you need to learn money-saving shopping strategies—and in the case of appliances and electronics, maintenance tips to prolong the life of your purchase. Here are big ways to save on big-ticket items.

appliances

Big-ticket items like appliances don't have to take a big bite out of your budget. Once you know how to shop for refrigerators, ranges, washing machines, and other appliances, you can beat retailers at their own game—and get a great bargain in the process.

how can you get a good deal on an appliance?

- Do your homework. Study the circulars in Sunday's papers to find out who's having a sale on your particular appliance—and what the sale price is—and surf the Web for appliance deals as well. (Try mysimon.com, nextag.com, and ebay.com as well as manufacturers' Web sites for a full range of comparative prices.) Then go to your local appliance store and ask the sales rep to match the deal you found elsewhere, including delivery charges and sales tax.

- Buy more than one appliance at a time. For example, if you purchase a washing machine and dryer together, you may be able to negotiate a better price than if you had bought them separately. You'll reduce delivery charges, too.

- Don't give up if the sales rep won't at first match your deal. Ask for a free extended warranty and free accessories—and then ask to speak to the manager to lower the price, keeping the freebies you just earned.

- Keep your eyes peeled for minor imperfections in the appliance you want. A small nick or dent on a new appliance may mean dollars off for you.

- If you find a better deal before your appliance is delivered, call the salesperson and ask if he can match the lower price.

- Try to shop at an appliance store or department when it's empty. You're more likely to score a bargain when a salesperson is eager to make a sale.

not new? not bad!

- Like car dealers, appliance retailers discount their current inventory when new models arrive. You can find discounts

PENNY WISE, POUND FOOLISH

Don't ask for such a large discount that it destroys all possibility of the seller making a profit. Keep in mind that the retail prices of large appliances like refrigerators are usually marked up by 15 percent from the wholesale prices while smaller appliances like microwaves are marked up about 30 percent.

Refrigerators eat up the most electricity in the household. Maximize efficiency by keeping the fridge at 37° F and the freezer at 0° F.

as high as 20 to 40 percent off last year's models and styles of appliances—true bargains for savvy shoppers. If you're really canny, try to find out when the next year's new models will hit the showroom.

- Consider used, too. As long as the appliance isn't more than five years old, it can be a good deal. (An older appliance won't be as energy efficient as a current appliance and can hit your utility bills hard.) Just note that nicks and dents in used appliances (as opposed to new) could be a sign of trouble. (In fact, never buy a used refrigerator that has a bad smell or a loose gasket.) Make sure the appliance works—ask to see it in operation—before you take it home. Check out used-appliance stores, repair shops that may have unclaimed items, and estate sales.

- Reconditioned appliances that have been taken apart, cleaned, repaired, put back together, and tested can save you money, too. Search for "reconditioned appliances" online (you can look for resellers near you). Some of these resellers may stock appliances that were returned to manufacturers. Look for a 30-day guarantee from any reseller.

refrigerators

The best way to save money once you own a refrigerator is to keep it in tip-top shape. Maintaining your appliance will save you money on your utility bills and help keep repair costs down—or even avoid them altogether. Here's what to do:

- Vacuum or brush the refrigerator condenser coil every six months—more if you have pets—to cut your electricity bill (unless the manufacturer says otherwise). How? Simply unplug the appliance, snap off the grate that covers the coil, and thoroughly vacuum it or clean it with a brush that you can find at a hardware store.

- Wipe the rubbery gasket that surrounds the refrigerator door once a month, and rub petroleum jelly on the side with the hinges.

REPAIR OR REPLACE?

How do you know if you should pay to repair your appliance—or if you should spring for a new one? The Good Housekeeping Research Institute says that if your estimated repair bill is more than 40 to 50 percent of the cost of a new appliance (including delivery and installation), you should buy a new one—especially if your appliance is old. (Small countertop electric appliances are not usually worth the expense to repair.)

- Make sure you have plenty of food in your freezer; a less-than-full freezer has to work harder to stay cold. Try to keep it at least ⅔ full to help the appliance operate more efficiently. Fill it with plastic containers of water if it's empty.

ranges

The best way to save money on your range is to save money on the energy used to heat it. These tips will help you do just that.

- Cook more than one dish at a time, such as a roast and baked potatoes, to make your oven more efficient.

- Preheat only when necessary and for no longer than needed. There's no need to preheat the oven for large roasts and other long-cooked foods.

- Avoid frequent door openings. They waste energy, allow heat to escape, and result in longer cooking times.

- Turn off the oven a few minutes before the cooking time is over. Residual heat will allow the food to continue cooking at the proper temperature until it's done.

- For stove-top efficiency, put pots and pans on similar-size burners. Small pots on big burners waste energy and are a safety hazard while large pots on small burners will not heat evenly.

microwave ovens

Though your microwave oven is not the priciest appliance you own, it's still worth maintaining to make it last. And the best way to keep your microwave working is to keep it clean.

- Spray an all-purpose cleaner onto a sponge and wipe up any messes in the microwave.

- Don't spray the cleaner directly on the oven—you may get moisture into the vents, which can damage the appliance.

- Be sure to clean up spills and splatters right after they happen: a dirty microwave doesn't cook as well as a clean one. (The splatters will absorb some of the microwave energy you need to heat your food.)

washing machines

You'll find a wide variety of washing machines on the market—ranging from front loaders that can handle bulky items like comforters to top loaders that easily handle your family's laundry. Here's how to get the best deal on the best washer for you:

- Buy a white washer. Designer colors add to the cost of the machine, not to the quality.

SAVING $ SAVES THE ENVIRONMENT

• **Look for products with the Energy Star label** when shopping for a new appliance. The star says that the appliance meets strict energy efficiency guidelines set by the U.S. Environmental Protection Agency and the U.S. Department of Energy. These energy-efficient appliances can save you up to 20 percent on your utility bills.

• **Look for the yellow energy guide label** when comparing the same type of appliance. This guide tells you how energy efficient the appliance is, how its energy use compares to that of similar products, and how much it will cost to run for a year. Remember that a highly efficient, more expensive refrigerator can cost you less than a less efficient, less expensive model over its lifetime.

• Stick to the basics. Extra bells and whistles won't necessarily give you better cleaning performance, just more options and features.

• Consider front-loading washing machines. They use less water, less detergent, and less energy than the traditional top-loading machines.

• Among top-loading machines, search for ones without agitators. They use less water and detergent than their traditional counterparts. A typical energy-saving washer uses 18 to 25 gallons of water per load, while a typical standard top-loading machine uses 40 gallons. In general, look for a low WF (water factor), which measures the amount of water used, and a high MEF (modified energy factor), which measures the energy efficiency of the appliance.

REPAIR AND SAVE

Have you noticed some water around your washer?
Here's how you can stop this little problem from turning into an expensive disaster:

• **The easy fix:** Check the water hoses connected to the back of the machine—the leak is most likely coming from a small crack in the rubber. If so, you'll need to replace the faulty hoses immediately, before a major break occurs. Turn off the water supply (so you won't come home to a flood) and buy new hoses at any hardware store or home center. To install, unscrew and remove the old hoses, then screw the new ones in and tighten with a wrench.

• **Pro tip:** Professional plumbers recommend that you buy steel braided hoses—they're more expensive but also more durable.

If the hoses aren't the problem, a service call may be necessary.

dryers

There are several tricks you can use to save money on dryers. Use some when you buy the dryer, and some to maintain it to save money over its lifetime.

- Buy a white dryer. You can find lots of designer-colored dryers, but they can add about $100 to the cost of the machine. You'll get the same features and performance in white.

- Look for a basic dryer. Choose one in the same line as a dryer with lots of bells and whistles—you'll often get the same performance as the fancier dryer at a much lower cost.

- Use the automatic cycle whenever you can. Most dryers today have sensors that stop the machine when the clothes are dry. If you set the dryer for 60 minutes, you may be drying your already dry clothes for 10 unnecessary minutes, which isn't good for either the clothes or your utility bill.

- Keep the lint screen free of lint.

- Make sure the dryer vents outside are clean.

- Check outside for birds' nests and debris at the end of the vent. Clean everything out; material in the vent will slow down the dryer's performance and can be a fire hazard.

vacuum cleaners

Saving money on a vacuum doesn't end when you buy the vacuum. You need to maintain it for a longer life.

- For the best suction, change the bag when it looks about two thirds full. If you have a bagless model, empty the dirt container after you've used the vacuum twice.

- Clean the filter from the dust cup of a bagless vacuum once a month—either tap it clean or, for best results, rinse it if possible. Check other filters once or twice a year on all vacuums and clean or replace them.

THINK TWICE

If an appliance doesn't work, check to make sure it is plugged in and all controls are properly set before calling for service. You'll save the repairman's time and your money.

electronics

Saving money on electronics—televisions, DVD players, stereo receivers, MP3 players, and computers—may seem difficult, since the prices seem to change as often as the technology. But if you stick to a few simple rules, you can become a savvy shopper in this area, too.

televisions

- If you're in the market for a new TV, spring's the time to shop and save. You may find one of last year's models on sale before the new ones fill the shelves.

- Don't pay extra for a top-of-the-line TV if you don't need all the bells and whistles. If you don't want or don't like surround-sound, for example, don't buy a TV with inputs for it.

- Likewise, don't pay for internal features—like a DVD player—if you already have the same features externally.

UNPLUG AND SAVE

Unplug unused electronics. Surprisingly, the electronic devices that stay on even when not in use—computers, TVs, cell phone chargers, and so on—add about 4 percent to your electricity bill. You can save about $30 a year if you simply unplug what you don't use.

SHOP SMART

Save money on electronics by shopping online with these tips in mind:

• **Search for the product name** and the words "coupon" or "promotional code" before you place an order. You may find a sale on what you're looking for or an offer for free shipping.

• **Don't forget that some chains let you buy** your product online and then pick it up at the store. This way you can avoid hefty shipping charges while still getting a good deal on the Web.

dvd players

• Do you have to pay top dollar for a top quality DVD player? The answer is a resounding "no." Look for color clarity, contrast, and the amount of space the DVD player takes up—as well as price.

• As with a TV, don't pay for fancy extra features if you won't use them.

stereo receivers and mp3 players

- Be realistic about your needs when you buy a receiver. Don't spend money on extra inputs and outputs if you don't plan on using them.

- When a new MP3 player is introduced, get last year's model number and buy that model from a retailer's extra inventory. Because turnover is so fast in this field, an older model is just as good as the newest generation, minus one or two features.

computers

- Buy a laptop for your home office. It uses considerably less power than a desktop computer.

- Computer manufacturers routinely add new features to their monitors—features you may not need. If you're not planning to hook your computer up to your TV, for example, don't pay for the feature that allows you to do that. Stick to what you need and you'll pay less.

- Cartridges are the big cost, not the printer. Don't forget to factor in the cost of the cartridges when you shop for a printer.

- Once printer ink cartridges have outlived their usefulness, they can save you a few dollars: next time you buy something at Staples, turn in your cartridge and get a discount (usually $3) on your purchase.

- Many cartridges are reusable. They can be refilled with toner, rather than replaced.

- Configure your printer so that it prints on both sides of the page, if possible.

- Recycle paper. You know those extra pages you sometimes get when printing out one simple e-mail? Turn them over and put them back in the printer for reuse. Saving that paper will save you money. And don't toss all those school papers that clutter your house. If they're blank on the back, put them in the printer for less important printouts.

- The best way to keep your printer in top working order— and prolong its life—is by using a dust cover.

SAVING $ SAVES THE ENVIRONMENT

What should you do with your computer once it has outlived its usefulness? Don't dump it, since it's not biodegradable and its mercury and lead can poison water supplies. Instead, help the environment while you help yourself to some savings.

• **Trade it.** Dell (dell.com), HP (hp.com), and Gateway (gateway.com) will take your outdated computer—from any manufacturer—and apply the value of the old computer toward one of their newer models.

• **Recycle it.** Dell will dispose of your computer in an environmentally-friendly way. Dell accepts any kind of computer, keyboard, mouse, monitor, or printer—and best of all, Dell will pick it up at your door. HP has a similar program, too.
  You can also visit earth911.org: this non profit organization offers a detailed listing of recycling centers, including those that specialize in computers. Enter your zip code to find the center nearest you.
  Check your state environmental agency's Web site for listings of electronic recyclers as well as your community's recycling or hazardous waste service. Check your local government's Web site or the government pages of your phone book for information.

• **Sell it**. Ask computer stores if they buy old computers. You won't make a fortune, but you'll be able to get rid of your computer with a good conscience.

SAVING $ SAVES THE ENVIRONMENT

• **Donate it.** Give your working computer to any number of charitable organizations and you'll get a tax deduction in return. Contact Share the Technology (sharetechnology.org); they'll match you with a non-profit organization that needs computer equipment.

You can also donate it through Dell (dell.com) and HP (hp.com) via the National Cristina Foundation, which helps disabled and economically disadvantaged people in your area. The Foundation will pick up the computer at your home.

HOW TO NEGOTIATE

You: Oh, I see the box for this printer has been opened.

Them: Yes, but all the parts are there and in perfect working order. There's nothing wrong with it.

You: Hmmm . . . I don't think anyone is going to be willing to pay full price for an item that has already been opened. Do you think you could mark it down 10 percent?

Them: Well, I don't know . . .

You: I'd be willing to pay the total in cash, today.

food

Whether you eat to live or live to eat, food is a big recurring expense. Here are ways to save on groceries, restaurant meals, takeout food, and cooking at home.

groceries

Groceries are a significant household expense. You can, however, greatly reduce your grocery bill by applying a few simple strategies to your trips to the supermarket.

before you head to the store

- Coupons are your first weapon in the battle of the supermarket budget. Use the money-saving guidelines for coupons in How to Be a Smart Shopper (see page 11) to help you cut up to 50 percent off your shopping bill.

- Don't forget to join the free frequent-shopper program at every store where you shop. These incentive programs can reduce your grocery bill by up to 10 percent.

- Use the store's circulars to plan your menu for the week.

- Combine weekly specials with cost-cutting coupons.

- Make a list of what you need, and stick to what's on your list: impulse shopping can cause serious shock at the cash register.

SHOPPING SEDUCERS

- **Ignore the shelves at eye-level,** particularly those on the right-hand side: they typically hold the most expensive items. Instead, check out shelves above and below where you would normally look.

- **Avoid the child-size shopping cart.** It is the perfect storage place for all the goodies your child may pull from the eye-level shelves.

- **Don't hurry to buy items** advertised as "Hurry, while supplies last!" Chances are, there isn't a shortage. And don't believe you *have* to buy 10 items if the limit you can buy is 10. Grocers can increase sales by as much as 105 percent by claiming a shortage and setting a high limit on the amount of a sale item you can buy.

- **Don't feel obligated to buy two items** just because they're advertised together. Unless otherwise indicated, ads that say "Buy two for $5" don't mean you *have* to buy two. If you want only one, buy only one for $2.50.

- Shop only once a week to avoid recurring impulse purchases.

- Take your mother's advice and never go to the store hungry. You'll be less likely to buy food you don't need.

- Identify which markets routinely offer you the best deals on specific products and buy them at those markets.

- For one month, jot down the highest and lowest prices your supermarket charges on the major items you buy each week. That way, when a price hits bottom and you have a coupon, you know it's the right time to buy 10.

money-saving tips in the shopping aisle

- Compare unit prices of products, not just the total price— you'll be amazed how illusory packaging can be.

- Stock up on nonperishable products on sale that you frequently use, such as toilet paper, paper towels, cleaning supplies, and canned goods. Check expiration dates—even on items like tea that you think won't ever expire, because they may.

- Buy in bulk when possible (after making sure that the unit price is indeed less on the bulk buy), but don't buy huge quantities of products you're not absolutely sure you'll use. It's better to buy fewer at a higher price than throw away many you got for a "deal." Good bulk purchases include cereal, rice, beans, pasta, flour, sugar, aluminum foil, toilet paper, and paper towels.

- Skip boxed frozen vegetables and buy large frozen bags instead. They generally cost less per serving.

Some items at the warehouse club may not actually be cheaper than those at the grocery store—especially if you plan to use coupons at the market.

- Buy fruits and vegetables that are in season—they often cost less than their out-of-season cousins—and look for sales on produce as well. Buy both ripe and almost-ripe produce so that it will be less likely to go bad before you're ready to eat it.

- Buy dried, rather than fresh, versions of products like beans and pasta.

- Steer clear of premade, prewashed, and convenience foods. You'll pay a premium for store-made meatloaf, bagged salad greens, and ready-to-eat vegetables.

- Likewise, you can pay 50 percent less for foods that don't already have sugar, spices, or sauces mixed in. So shop for ingredients to make your own marinades, seasonings, and baking mixes rather than paying for premade.

- Remember that premixed juice can cost 60 percent more than frozen concentrate.

- Pay $1 less per five-pound bag of granulated sugar than for pure cane sugar. They're interchangeable, whether baking a cake or adding a teaspoon to morning coffee.

- Double-check the weight of heavy items, like a five-pound bag of onions or a ten-pound bag of apples. Make sure you're getting what you're paying for.

- Buy larger cuts of meat. Bigger pieces of meat often cost less per pound than smaller pieces. Ask your butcher to cut beef rump, bottom round, or beef chuck shoulder into smaller pieces; freeze what you're not using right away.

- Look for family packs of meat at the grocery store or big packages of meat at the warehouse store. Again, label and freeze what you're not using immediately.

- Choose bone-in pieces of less tender meats. Not only will they cost less, they'll also add greater flavor to soups, stews, and slow-cooker dishes. Try lamb shanks, veal breast, chuck blade steaks, and shoulder lamb chops.

- Don't ignore cuts of meat with fat. Leaner cuts tend to be more expensive. Look instead for beef chuck, fresh ham, and cross-rib pot toast; they're tender and juicy after a long braise, and you can skim off the fat after cooking.

- Looking for bargain beef? Flat iron steak is well marbled

and so tender—it's considered the second most tender cut of beef—that it doesn't need a marinade. Best of all, it's a great value. Flat iron steak might also be called beef shoulder top blade steak (flat iron). Either way, it's a rectangular steak that weighs about 7 ounces and is ¾ to 1¼ inches thick.

- Other value cuts include shoulder center steak (ranch cut), shoulder petite tender, round sirloin tip center steak, and bottom round steak (Western griller).

- Avoid nongrocery items, like shampoo, body lotion, and vitamins, at the grocery store. You can pay up to 25 percent more for toiletries there than at a drugstore.

- Check out the discount aisle before you head to the check-out counter. You can find slightly damaged cereal boxes, ready-to-eat fruits and vegetables, and day-old bakery goods for a lot less than their perfect counterparts.

- Ask customer service for a rain check if the store has run out of an advertised item. This written promise to sell you that item at the advertised price when it's back in stock can save you plenty. Just be sure the rain check outlines the sale price, the number of items you can buy at the sale price, and when the rain check expires.

- Buy only what you'll use—don't buy something simply because it's on sale.

at the register

- Check the register prices. Scanners are not always right, whether it's the cashier's register or one on a self-checkout line. Too often a special promotional price on the shelf has not been input into the register.

- To help remember which of your products should be discounted, put the specially-priced items together on the checkout counter, so you can keep track of the prices as the items are being scanned.

- Speak up if the scanner makes a mistake! Whether it's an error on the price of the product or on what the product is—domestic cheddar cheese versus imported romano—be sure to note the proper price. At some big chains you may even get the item for free if the scanner displays a higher price than the one advertised.

shop outside your grocery store

- Broaden your horizons beyond your favorite market. If you shop by what's on sale at several different stores, you can save plenty. Cherry-picking—the term for shopping at different stores for items on sale—can save a bundle (even with the price of gas factored in).

- Shop at less-traditional venues, too. Do some of your shopping at a warehouse club—to avoid waste, split your purchases with a friend—and you'll more than save your annual fee.

PENNY WISE, POUND FOOLISH

Don't stock up on ready-to-serve orange juice when it's on sale. Researchers have found that oxygen destroys the vitamin C in ready-to-serve orange juice, even while it's in the store waiting to be sold. And the vitamin C content dips further once you open the container—it could even drop to zero, depending on how long it sits on your refrigerator shelf. So what's a savvy shopper to do?

1. Buy orange juice that won't expire for three or four weeks, and drink it within a week of bringing it home.

2. Better yet, buy frozen concentrate. It has about 25 percent more vitamin C per serving than ready-to-serve, and it won't lose its vitamin C content until you mix it with water. Best of all, frozen concentrate costs less than ready-to-serve.

- Don't forget to shop at mass retailers. You can save a bundle by shopping for snacks at Target, for example.

- Think about joining a food co-op, where consumers jointly buy groceries in bulk. You may have to work there a few hours a month to be a member, but you can save up to 15 percent on your total bill in return. Check out coopdirectory.org to find a co-op near you.

- Buy in-season fruits and vegetables at a local farmer's market, and shop there at the end of the day when vendors often reduce prices to avoid taking home their food. (There are nearly 4,000 farmers' markets in the United States, double the number from ten years ago.) You can find one near you by logging on to ams.usda.gov/farmersmarkets.

- Do you prefer grocery shopping online for convenience?

  1. You may be able to get a substantial discount for trying a particular online grocery service for the first time.

  2. For additional savings, check your online grocer's money-saving policies. The online grocer may let you use another grocer's frequent buyer card, accept valid manufacturers' coupons, and offer specials and coupons.

  3. If you want to buy in bulk online to save money, go to bythecase.net for places to buy what you need in big quantities.

WHO KNEW?

Timing your grocery shopping can save you money. Try shopping in the morning when baked goods from the day before are on sale. You'll find fresher produce then, too.

restaurants

Eating out is one of life's great pleasures, but it inevitably—and obviously—comes with a price tag. Here are smart ways to cut the cost of eating at your favorite restaurants.

- Drink tap water instead of ordering soft drinks, coffee, or bottled water to cut your dinner bill by as much as 20 percent.

- Order a variety of appetizers as your meal; they're less expensive and often just as filling as entrees. Try to coordinate the time of your meal with the time the restaurant serves appetizers at half price.

- Wait until you get home for coffee and dessert. There's a high markup on both.

- Share family-style dishes rather than ordering smaller, individual portions that tend to cost more.

- Pay attention to special promotions for children (kids eat free night), seniors—even teachers!

- Take advantage of early bird specials. They offer substantial savings, and you don't have to be a particular age to enjoy them.

- If you're not very hungry and can't take home leftovers, order a half portion. It's cheaper and you won't waste food. (If you can take home leftovers, order a full portion and enjoy your leftovers the next day.)

- Collect restaurant coupons from weekend newspapers and your daily mail (in the form of freestanding postcards, envelopes full of offers, and magazine-style collections of coupons). You can find deals for dollars off your meal, a percentage off your total bill, and even buy-one-get-one-free offers. Just watch for restrictions on days and times of use. (See coupons, page 12 for more information.)

- Think about buying the Entertainment Book (entertainmentbook.com) for worthwhile savings. Coupons in local editions range from fast food to casual dining and offer dollars-off as well as buy-one-get-one-free offers. In addition, if you register your book online you can print out additional coupons. Just be sure that the restaurants you like are featured in the book with times and days you like before you buy it.

- Use search engines such as Google to your advantage. Type in the name of a restaurant followed by "coupon" to see if your desired restaurant offers any printable coupons.

- Find discount certificates on restaurant.com. Type in your zip code to find restaurants offering dollars-off certificates for a small fee. For example, get a $25 certificate for $10—but watch for restrictions including minimum purchase, which meal you can use it for, and which days you can use it.

- Participate in the Rewards Network (rewardsnetwork.com). Here's how it works: you pay $49 a year and register a credit or debit card on the site. When you use that particular card at one of thousands of participating restaurants, you'll receive cash back—up to 20 percent of the bill will be credited to your next credit or debit card statement.

- Tired of spending a fortune on lunch just so you can catch up with your co-workers, but don't feel like brown-bagging it every day? Try taking turns bringing lunch for co-workers. You'll get a great variety of dishes—and save a bundle.

- Here's a solution for those days when you don't want to cook but don't want to spend money at a restaurant, either: buy a ready-made meal from your local grocery store. Many grocery stores now sell high-quality premade dishes like sushi, chicken francese, and meat- and vegetable lasagna. One of these supermarket meals could cost only about a quarter of a restaurant meal.

takeout

Depending on your tastes, bringing restaurant food home to eat can be as expensive as eating out. The biggest tip for curbing these costs? Don't take out. Here are ways to avoid spending the family food budget on takeout.

- Give up pizza once a month— eat it just two weeks instead of four—and save $200 in a year.

- Skip the cappuccino and order coffee with milk instead. You could save about $2 a cup—a hefty savings just for leaving out a little foam.

- If you take coffee singles (they look like tea bags but are filled with coffee) to work rather than buy your morning fix at the coffee shop on the way, you can save more than $300 in one year.

- If you want to avoid the cost of takeout, cook two meals at a time: one for dinner and another for the freezer. That way you'll always have a nutritious dinner at the ready when you're tired, hungry, and short on time.

- Buy in bulk with a group of families (split the cost of groceries) and then prepare meals together. Spend part of a weekend day chopping and cooking and dividing the meals for freezing, and you'll have dinners for much of the month—as well as a lot of fun. Visit 30daygourmet.com for bulk cooking recipes and shopping lists.

- Too busy to cook? Now you don't have to fall back on expensive takeout food. Instead, pick up half a dozen or more meals in one trip at one of the many meal-prep businesses sprouting up across the country. Chains like Dream Dinners and Super Suppers run commercial kitchens that cook a wide variety of entrées and side dishes, such as roast pork with potatoes au gratin and grilled mahimahi with couscous and baby spring vegetables. You order online, go to the kitchen to assemble and label your meals, then take them home to your refrigerator or freezer. Prices typically run about $3 to $4 a serving or $12 to $16 per meal for a family of four.

money-saving meal ideas

You've saved at restaurants and avoided takeout—but you can save more with these easy-to-implement tips for preparing food at home. (Be sure to read money–saving tips in the shopping aisle on page 120 as well.)

- Ditch the salad dressing from the store and make your own. Even if you use the finest ingredients available for a vinaigrette, you'll save more than $2 per cup.

- Keep leftover chicken pieces in a heavy-duty bag in the freezer. When the bag is full, make your own stock.

- Grow your own herbs. Plant rosemary, thyme, marjoram, and sage—the easiest to grow—in small pots on your kitchen windowsill. If you're a little more ambitious, plant basil, mint, and chives in your outdoor garden in late spring.

- Always eat breakfast at home. Whatever you eat will be less expensive than going out.

BUDGET-FRIENDLY MEALS

Looking for ways to save at the dinner table? Try these easy, economical, and crowd-pleasing meals.

- Spaghetti with marinara sauce
- Chicken noodle soup
- Macaroni and cheese
- Tuna noodle casserole
- Fish and chips
- Oven-fried chicken with coleslaw
- Grilled chicken over leafy greens
- Homemade pizza
- Vegetarian chili
- Omelets
- Franks and beans
- Chicken-fried steak
- Buffalo chicken wings
- Taco salad
- Black bean quesadillas

- Store grains and cereals in the refrigerator to increase their shelf life. This is an especially good idea in warm weather.

- Save hundreds of dollars per year by pureeing your own baby food. Simply add several spoonfuls of your cooked dinnertime vegetables into a blender and process until smooth.

- Add deli meats to your dinner. Shred or cube a thick slice of deli ham, roast beef, or roast turkey and use it in pasta or stir-fry dishes rather than serve a larger meat dish.

- Cook a meal without meat at least once a week. Don't forget to include protein-rich foods like whole grains, tofu, and beans in your meatless meals.

- Give up bottled water. If you can't, install a home water cooler. Once you've paid the hefty initial cost, you'll pay significantly less for water compared to the bottles you used to buy.

BEST OF THE WEB: housewares

cooking.com This kitchenwares site offers discounts on well-known brands like All-Clad, Calphalon, and Kitchen Aid. Check out the clearance section.

replacements.com Trying to find serving pieces that match your grandmother's silver tableware? Need to replace the china cup your four-year-old broke at her imaginary tea party? Look no further. This site stocks eleven million pieces from more than 250,000 patterns going back 100 years.

King Arthur (kingarthurflour.com) Bakers on the search for special flours know about King Arthur, but the site also sells hard-to-find ingredients like organic barley malt syrup and a wide selection of housewares.

SAVING $ SAVES THE ENVIRONMENT

Teach kids to be green. Give your little ones responsibility for your family's recycling and match whatever they make in deposits at the store. They'll learn about money and recycling at the same time.

- Make your own iced tea. Use fruit juice for flavor.

- Buy small juice boxes for young children; they rarely finish all the juice in the bigger boxes that cost more.

fashion and beauty

Sometimes half the fun of looking good is in shopping for the right clothes, shoes, and makeup, and getting your hair done perfectly. The other half comes from finding a bargain in all these areas, which is easy to do with the tips in this chapter.

clothing

What woman doesn't love shopping for clothes? And who doesn't love a great bargain? Here are fun and frugal strategies for buying the clothes you love at a fraction of what you've spent in the past.

finding fashion frugally

- Stock up on frequent-buyer cards. Even better than the card that gives you a free DVD rental after renting 10 movies, these cards reward you with discounts when you spend money on clothes and accessories at their store. With Delia's Frequent Buyer Card, for example, spend $200 and you'll get $20 off your next purchase of $20 or more.

- Use those store credit cards (wisely). If you can control your purchases, store credit cards offer a great deal: use them when you shop, and get coupons in the mail for serious money to apply to your next purchase. Many store credit cards give you a discount on your first purchase with the card (often 10 percent), and some offer promotions that allow you to buy items and defer payment for 90 days. Just be sure to find out about the interest rate before you sign up. Some cards' rates can be extremely high.

- Think ahead when shopping from catalogs or online. If there's even the slightest chance that you'll have to return what you bought, buy your clothes from catalogs and Web sites that let you return purchases to their bricks-and-mortar counterparts. That way you avoid return-shipping charges, which can get costly.

- Pay attention to shopping cycles. Stores replace their merchandise on a regular basis, putting outdated items on serious sale. If you figure out when the cycle ends, you can find some major deals. If you can determine the exact day the sale begins (and the store clerks will tell you), shop the day ahead and put the item you love on hold.

- Check out off-price catalogs and Web sites. Look for ones that sell not-quite-perfect merchandise—you'll get a bargain and often a perfectly good item at the same time. *Good Housekeeping* textiles experts, for example, had trouble finding imperfections in "slightly imperfect" hosiery for sale at onehanesplace.com.

- Many manufacturers use their Web sites to push sale and clearance items. Always check the sites of your favorite clothing and accessory maker for a sale section.

- Try sites that offer discounts on multiple brands as well, like bluefly.com. You can find discounted clothing, handbags, shoes, and accessories at this easy-to-navigate site.

- Use online shopping tips (see page 27) for all your clothes shopping.

- Organize a clothing exchange. Ask your friends to bring over their gently-used clothes and accessories that no longer fit, that they no longer love, or that never looked quite right. Separate the offerings into categories such as dresses, boots, and accessories and allow time for all guests to check out the treasures. Then have the hostess hold up each piece; anyone who wants that particular item raises her hand. If more than one guest covets a piece, have each interested shopper model it for the group. The group then votes on who should take the item home. At the end of the party guests can swap freely with others.

- Sign up for savings. You can get automatic e-mail updates from retailers like Gap and Old Navy or from your favorite online retailers. They'll send you e-mails with special money-saving offers and news about sales, special shopping events, and current merchandise.

- Sometimes you can save money on a perfectly good item simply by asking the manager for a discount. Tell her you adore that blouse, but it's a little too much of a stretch for you; could she discount it a bit? The worst she can say is no, and she might even say yes.

HOW TO NEGOTIATE

You: I notice there's a makeup stain right here, on the collar.

Them: I'm certain that will come off with a little club soda.

You: *Blink rapidly, say nothing.*

Them: I'll ask the manager what we can do about it.

- Don't be afraid to ask for a discount on a less-than-perfect piece of clothing or accessory you see. Whether it's a spot of makeup on a fabulous blouse or a small scuff on a leather belt, you may save up to 25 percent off the retail price. How? Simply tell the salesperson you want to buy the item but that it's damaged. She may offer you a 10 percent discount; don't accept immediately, since she may give you an even better deal if she thinks you're still on the fence.

- You know that sinking feeling you get when the pants you just bought go on sale the very next day? Here's an easy way to get over it. Take your receipt back to the store where you bought the pants and ask for the difference. Some stores will happily accommodate you if you do it within about two weeks after you made the purchase.

- Losing your luggage on a flight is always a bad experience, but checking out the contents of someone else's unclaimed baggage—and buying it—can be a terrific money saver. For example, visit unclaimedbaggage.com for a small selection of the goods available at the Unclaimed Baggage Center in Scottsboro, AL. You can also join their e-mail list, and they'll alert you to shipments of items you might like as well as notify you about online auctions and special sales.

- Make a shopping list—and stick to it. If your daughter needs jeans, buy jeans—not the cool capris in the next aisle she thinks she needs, even though she has several pairs. You should make a list for yourself and stick to it as well.

- Buy ahead on sale. If you see a great deal on clothes for you or clothes that will definitely fit your kids at a later date—T-shirts, shorts with elastic waistbands, light jackets—snap them up. Just be sure not to buy kids' clothes that require a perfect fit; your children may not grow into them perfectly.

- Let your kids grow with their clothes. Buy shirts and pants a little big and cuff them. Overalls with adjustable shoulder straps give longer wear. And don't forget that pants with elastic waists will see kids through their different shapes as they age.

- Organize a kids' clothing exchange. Get friends and relatives together to swap outgrown children's clothes. You can make it an informal exchange, or formalize the process with points (a coat is worth more points than a pair of pants, for example). Donate all leftover clothing to charity.

- Save on back-to-school savings. It's tempting to buy your kids all their new school clothes before classes start, but you should wait. Buy your children one or two new outfits; let them go to school to see what the trends are, then go back to buy what they really want—and what they'll really wear. Remember that retailers start discounting fall clothes a few weeks after school starts, so if you're patient you'll get better deals than those offered in back-to-school sales.

SCHOOL SAVINGS

• **Save money on school supplies** by buying pencils, pens, tape, and notebooks in bulk at an office-supply store. You'll save a bundle and won't have to run out to buy another item every time your child remembers at the last minute that he needs something for school.

• **Start looking for sales on school supplies early in the summer.** Office-supply stores often advertise sales long before school starts to get you into their stores.

- Go secondhand for your teen. Plato's Closet, a chain of 170 stores specializing in clothing that's gently used, caters to the young 20s, teen, and tween markets with trendy brands like American Eagle Outfitters and Abercrombie & Fitch. Clothing averages $10 an item, is in good condition, and, more importantly, is in style (as opposed to the outdated offerings at many secondhand stores).

thrift stores

Stores like the Salvation Army are treasure troves for real bargains, especially clothes for small children. You can find clean, attractive clothes for a fraction of their original cost. See consignment shopping (below) for tips that also apply to thrift store shopping.

consignment shopping

- Regularly check out consignment stores, where you'll find gently worn designer duds for one third the cost of retail. In addition, most consignment shops will reduce the price of their goods by 20 percent after one month, and an additional 20 to 30 percent after two months. You can even find new items here, since some boutiques, cloth- ing chains, and even designers consign their clothes to these shops at the end of each season.

- Set up a wish list. Let the store owner know you're dying for a particular Armani skirt, and ask to be called when it arrives. Be sure to pick it up immediately; stores generally won't hold items longer than one day.

- Put your name on the store's mailing list. You'll want to know if and when your store holds a "bag sale," where you get the chance to fill a shopping bag for a set amount (sometimes as little as $20).

- Do your homework. Check out department stores and fashionable boutiques to discover the prices of clothing you want. Write the prices down, and keep the list with you when you shop at consignment stores, so you'll know if you're really getting a price break. Web sites like eluxury.com will give you up-to-date prices as well.

- Be sure to try on all secondhand clothes before you buy. Some may have been altered, so the size tag may be meaningless—and all sales are final.

- Shop often—inventory is constantly changing—and particularly in January, February, July, and August, when stores discount prices up to 80 percent during end-of-season sales.

- Don't wait to buy the item you want. It may not be there on your return trip.

- Ask about the delivery schedule. Try to arrive at the store when the merchandise arrives.

- Shop at the beginning of the week. People tend to drop off donations over the weekend, so Monday and Tuesday are your best bets for the best variety.

- Consider volunteering at your local consignment shop or consignment sales. You'll get first dibs on whatever arrives.

outlet shopping

- Spend a day at outlet stores, where you can find first-rate items from the current season, along with last season's fashions and overruns from many manufacturers. Many outlets feature garments made specifically for those outlets.

- Always try the item on before you buy it. Returning clothes to an outlet store isn't always as easy as returning them to a full-price store.

CEDAR MAGIC

There's no need to replace cedar that seems to have lost its scent. Simply sand the wood.

GARMENT BAG TRICK

Transform pretty white pillowcases into garment bags for your clothes. They're breathable—unlike dry-cleaning bags—and won't cling to your clothes. Simply cut a small slit in the top of the pillowcases and slip your hangers through them.

- Become familiar with the actual price of the designer clothes you love. Outlet stores don't always offer a great deal, and sometimes don't offer a deal at all.

accessories

- Breathe new life into a boring old shirt by replacing the buttons with a rainbow of new ones. Design your own mix of colors, shapes, and materials (just make sure that whatever you choose fits through the buttonhole). The simpler the shirt, the more impact the new buttons will have. P.S. Don't forget the cuffs!

- Always remove good-quality buttons before you discard a garment. You can use them to replace missing buttons on other pieces of clothing or to spruce up an ordinary-looking blouse.

- Bypass inexpensive 100 percent nylons in favor of a pair with at least 15 percent Lycra, a stretchier yarn that increases run-resistance.

- Visit mass retailers such as Target, Wal-Mart, and Kohl's for fashionable accessories at reasonable prices.

- Buy classic, timeless accessories and avoid super-trendy pieces. They'll last forever, saving you money over the long run.

- Don't forget that some top-notch retailers offer free repairs or free tailoring. Coach, for example, provides free repairs for the life of the product (although there is a $20 shipping and handling fee).

BUYER BEWARE

Whether you get free repairs may depend on where you bought the item. Check the store and manufacturer's repair policies. Also, if the manufacturer offers a lifetime warranty, find out which lifetime it covers—yours or the product's.

HOW TO NEGOTIATE

You: I'd really love to buy this watch, but this is more than I'm willing to pay.

Them: We have several less expensive watches in this case over here. I'd be happy to show them to you.

You: But I love this one. Would you be willing to take 25 percent off the price? If you need to ask your manager, I'll just browse.

● Check out unusual places to shop for accessories. Try an Army/Navy store, a children's store, a drugstore (for pantyhose), and a hardware store (for canvas belts).

● Think you can bargain only with big-city sidewalk vendors for jewelry? Think again. Salespeople who work in jewelry stores with fancy displays are often willing to negotiate. Their necklaces, rings, bracelets, and other items are generally marked up by at least 100 percent, so they have lots of wiggle room on the price. Here's how to bargain: browse through the store for a while, ask questions about the item you want—including the list price—and then say, "Is this the best you can do?" Turn down the first offer and see if the salesperson comes up with an even better deal.

- Make an expensive-looking pendant by suspending a charm bracelet from a chain. Take a look in your jewelry box to see what great combos you can create with stuff you already have.

- Found a bargain on a watch you love? Just be sure that it (and any other discounted electronic gadget you buy) comes with a warranty.

shoes

Saving money on shoes doesn't just mean bypassing the $400 designer heels. Check out the following shoe strategies to save big while still putting your best foot forward.

- Buy your shoes online. You'll find a greater choice of color and size and you can save 10 to 15 percent over store prices, especially when shipping is free. (Some sites even offer free shipping on returns.) Try zappos.com, shoemall.com, shoebuy.com, and shoes.com for great selections and prices.

- Shop off-season for boots and sandals. You'll be amazed by the deals you can find.

- Love those sandals and slingbacks but worry that they're looking a little too worn? Instead of buying new shoes, ask your shoe repair expert to clean the insole sock lining—the leather base you slide your foot onto. Cleaning and repairing this part of your sandal or other summer-style shoe gives it a complete makeover.

- Replace worn heels. Your shoes will look better and last longer and you'll be amazed by the transformation.

- Request rubber soles next time your get your shoes repaired. They'll last longer.

- Women can renew their love for a forgotten pair of shoes by giving them a feminine flourish. Tie a grosgrain or satin ribbon onto a shoe clip, then slide the bow onto the front of the pump.

- Jazz up a neutral canvas shoe by adding a fun fabric pin or by simply replacing the standard-issue laces with colorful new ones or with ribbons. Anything goes (but nothing too wide). Size your new lace using the original as a guide.

- Buy inexpensive flip-flops and decorate them yourself.

- Salt stains can make shoes and boots look old before their time. To remove winter salt stains and dirt, mix equal parts of white vinegar and water or use a commercial desalter, and lightly sponge on smooth or grained leather shoes.

- When scrapes happen, it is sometimes possible to glue down peeled leather. If not, cover the spot with matching polish or indelible ink.

- Don't buy new boots just because your current pair looks old. Place empty plastic water or soda bottles upside-down inside your boots to stop the leather from drooping and creasing. To reduce odors and keep your boots smelling clean, put cedar chips or potpourri into the plastic bottles first, poke small holes in the bottles, then put the bottles in your boots.

- Try buying children's shoes for yourself. A child's size 5 translates into an adult's size 7—and is often one-third to one-half the price.

makeup

Considering the small size of makeup, the costs can seem large. But keep the following tips in mind and you'll find beauty in much less expensive packages.

- You don't need fancy makeup brushes to produce beautiful results. Here are three clever Q-tip makeup tricks:

  1. Enliven your eyes. Draw a light-brown shadow from lashline to crease with one end of the Q-tip. Use the other end of the swab to add a spot of gold or bronze shimmer to the inner corner of each eye.

  2. Erase mistakes. Turn the cotton swab into a handy eraser by dipping it into foundation. Use it to cover spots of mascara, uneven blush, and eyeliner problems.

  3. Sculpt cheekbones. Draw a curved line of gold eye shadow—applied with a Q-tip—from your temples to the apples of your cheeks. You will create cheekbones you never thought you had.

SUPER SITES: FREE STUFF ONLINE

Get coupons for the latest Procter & Gamble personal-care products on pg.com. Look under "Offers & Promotions."

- Many Web sites that carry beauty products offer free shipping, including drugstore.com, if you make a minimum purchase (usually $50).

- Check out keycode.com to find out about makeup promotions before you shop.

- Some stores (such as Ulta) send out sale notices and discounts via e-mail to club members. Be sure to enroll.

- Choose free samples when you make a purchase at Sephora.com. Search for "free samples" on the site's home page.

- Don't throw your makeup—and your money—away if you don't like what you've bought. You can return any cosmetic you don't like, even if you used it, at most major drugstore chains, including Rite Aid and Walgreens. They offer a money-back guarantee—just be sure to save your receipt.

- You spent the money, you love the shade, and now your broken lipstick is a goner—unless you can save it with this trick:

  1. Heat both sides of the broken bullet for five to six seconds (the Good Housekeeping Research Institute suggests using a hair dryer), until the product is pliable.

  2. Press the pieces together—gently.

  3. At the break, rub the sides of the lipstick in a circular motion to smooth and fill in the crack.

  4. Put the top on the tube and let it set for 20 minutes in your freezer.

  Presto! Good as new.

- If you spend money on a manicure or pedicure, get your nails painted with a light-colored polish: chips are much less obvious, so you can stretch out the time between applications.

- If you have a chip in your nail polish, soften the raised edges by smoothing on a drop of polish remover. Then apply polish to the chipped portion only. Once it dries, add another layer over the entire nail and follow up with top coat. If you have a French pedicure and it chips, cover the tip of the nail with Wite Out and then apply a clear coat of polish over it. No one will be any the wiser.

- With many expensive hand lotions, you're paying for perfume rather than moisture concentration. Consider switching to less expensive brands.

- Should you spend more for a fancy perfume? Do the high-end fragrances really last longer and smell better? Not always. You need to keep two things in mind when deciding on a costly scent: you're paying in part for the packaging and marketing, and a less expensive perfume may smell just as good if you feel fabulous wearing it.

hair care

No matter what kind of hair you have, you still have to spend money to maintain your mane and keep it looking good. Here are inexpensive ways to do that.

- Be a haircut model. Get your hair cut by a trainee at a hair salon and save big.

- Make sure you know the salon's policies before you get your hair done. Some salons charge extra for a blow dry at the end of a cut or coloring; skip it and save up to $20.

- Cut your kids' hair—and your spouse's too—for significant savings. For less than the price of one haircut you can buy *How to Cut Your Child's Hair at Home* by Laura Derosa, and for the cost of about two haircuts you can enlist the help of the Wahl Pro 26-Piece Haircut Kit (wahl-store.com), which includes the tools—scissors, comb, clippers, and more—you need as well as a DVD that shows you exactly what to do.

- Avoid layered haircuts and grow out the layers you already have. You'll need fewer trims.

services

We all need certain—often expensive—services in our everyday lives. The good news is that you *can* save money on phone service, health care, insurance, and credit cards. Check out the tips in the following pages to get good services for less.

phones

Though you may feel you have to pay whatever the phone company and your cell phone provider charge, there are ways around their seemingly inflexible cost structures. Just try the following.

landlines

- Though it's a good idea to keep a landline in case of emergency, you may not need to keep your long-distance plan. Drop the plan and use a prepaid phone card. You can call long distance for as little as three or four cents a minute—and there are no monthly service fees.

- Use your cell phone for long-distance calls, particularly on nights and weekends when many of these calls are free.

- If you feel more comfortable keeping your long-distance phone plan, call your carrier every six months to make sure it is giving you its best deal.

- Do you really need—or even use—all those extra phone services you're paying for? They really add up: call-waiting, call-forwarding, caller ID, and so on can tack up to $10 a month to your bill, even when they're part of your phone plan.

- Stop paying for the insurance from the phone company that covers the wire and jacks inside your house. The insurance, called basic wire maintenance, is optional—even though it routinely appears on your phone bill—and problems inside your house are rare.

- Get off the phone and on to the Web for directory assistance. Dialing 411 can cost you up to $1.50 per call, so instead go to a Web directory like switchboard.com or theultimates.com, which lets you search multiple directories at one time.

- Screen your calls with your answering machine, rather than with caller ID, and you'll save about $60 per year.

MAKE PHONE BATTERIES LAST LONGER

Here's how the Good Housekeeping Research Institute says you can prolong the life of your cordless phone batteries:

• **Follow the instructions for charging the battery completely as soon as you get your new phone home.** The initial charge can take up to 20 hours, and it's important that you don't interrupt the charge—you could permanently shorten the life of the battery.

• **Keep the phone away from radiators, the oven, and any other sources of heat**—including sunny spots in your house. Batteries get worn down by high temperatures.

cell phones

- Rethink your commitment to your cell phone provider. That two-year plan may give you a good deal on a cool new phone, but you'll probably be able to find a better plan during the second year of your contract.

- Skip lost-cell phone insurance coverage. You'll be charged $4 to $6 in monthly premiums, and you'll have to pay a deductible that ranges from $35 to $110. Plus, there's no guarantee that the replacement phone will be as good as the phone you lost. In fact, you may get a replacement that's used or refurbished. Chances are you can get a new phone with the features you want for less than the yearly cost of insurance combined with the deductible.

- When shopping for a cell-phone plan, add up the number of minutes you think you'll use each month and tack on 20 percent more minutes, just to be safe—because if you use more than your allotted minutes, you could wind up paying about seven times more per minute.

- Find out if cell phone providers offer a discount to employees at the company you work for.

- You may save money on your cell phone by buying it from an authorized retailer rather than from a wireless-service

BREAK YOUR CELL PHONE CONTRACT

Want to get out of a cell phone contract early without paying a termination fee of $200 or so? There are two possibilities:

1. Find someone who wants to take over your contract. The Web sites cellswapper.com and celltradeusa.com match cell owners with prospective buyers (your cost: up to $20). You might find someone who wants your particular model or needs a short-term cell phone plan. If you make a match—though there's no guarantee you will—your cell-service provider needs to broker the transfer.

2. Use the price-change loophole. Your cell phone service contract may let you out without a fee if the carrier announces a price change affecting your plan. So if your service provider sends you a letter about an upcoming fee revision, call the company immediately to try to cancel for free.

provider. Retailers make so much selling wireless service, some believe they can afford to make very little profit (or take a loss) on the phone.

- Want to avoid cell phone contract hassles altogether? Try a pay-as-you-go cell phone. You buy the phone and the minutes, and add minutes when you use up your current allotment. No fees, no taxes, no contracts—and most of the major providers offer them.

health care

Health care costs seem to keep rising, with no end in sight. Here are ways to keep a lid on your costs.

prevention

- Keep an eye out for free skin cancer screenings given by dermatologists and medical schools during Skin Cancer Awareness Month (May).

- Get screened free for kidney disease. Check out keeponline.org for a screening location near you.

- Ask your employer if it offers health screenings through its employee assistance programs. You may discover free screenings for skin cancer and more.

- Check local pharmacies for free blood pressure, cholesterol, and blood sugar checkups.

- Ask local dental schools if they offer free checkups.

- Exercise for health—less expensively. Check your health insurance policy for discounts on gyms. Many health insurers offer their members as much as 60 percent off certain health club memberships.

- Drop your gym membership; borrow workout tapes from the library and invest in hand weights.

- Get free testing for depression at medical schools, particularly on National Depression Screening Day, which usually falls in October.

prescriptions, supplements, and more

- Doctors often have samples of prescription drugs in their offices, courtesy of drug company representatives. Your doctor may offer you free samples of the drug you need; if she doesn't, simply ask if she has any.

- Try comparison shopping for your prescriptions. Chain drugstores, independent drugstores, and online pharmacies may charge wildly different prices for the same medicine. If you take more than one prescription, be sure to check the price of each individually; one pharmacy may not have the lowest price on all the prescriptions you need. If you buy your medications at several different pharmacies, be sure to ask each pharmacist about possible drug interactions.

- Prescription discount cards can work to your advantage. Many national chains—such as Target—offer pharmacy rewards cards that can save you money throughout the store. (Seniors qualify for special prescription discounts with a card at Rite Aid.) If you prefer your local independent pharmacy, ask if it offers a similar type of discount card (or a senior discount, if you qualify). The AARP has its own version—the AARP Rx Member Choice card (aarp.org; 877-231-6015) that costs $19.95 per year and can save you up to 53 percent on top-selling prescriptions.

- Look into the cost of your prescriptions at discount retailers like Wal-Mart, which offers over 350 prescription drugs for $4 each.

- Buy your prescription glasses at a warehouse club. You'll be amazed at the high quality and low price.

- Ask for a AAA discount on your prescription glasses and prescription sunglasses. Some eyeglass providers offer it.

- Ask your doctor if you can use a generic version of your prescription drugs. The savings can be significant.

- Look into mail-order prescriptions. Some insurance plans let you buy three months of medication via mail for the price of a single month.

- If your insurance plan doesn't cover oral contraceptives, buy them for half price at smartwomanrx.com, a site endorsed by the National Association of Nurse Practitioners in Women's Health. You can save up to $200 a year on three popular brands (Levlen, Tri-Levlen, and Levlite).

- Visit drugstore.com, where prices are routinely lower than those at drugstores, mass merchandisers, and warehouse clubs.

    1. Find coupons on the drugstore.com site to save even more.

    2. Get free samples by submitting your e-mail address.

    3. Look for rebates for your favorite brands.

    4. Check out promotional offers for free standard shipping on significant orders, and look for coupons on the site for free shipping on lower-priced orders.

    5. You'll save even more if you're a frequent shopper. Every three months, drugstore.com gives you a credit for five percent of the amount you've spent on nonprescription products that you can apply to the following month's bill.

- Avoid grocery stores when buying health care products like vitamins, unless you have a significant cents-off coupon. Grocery stores sometimes charge 25 percent more than drugstores for the same items.

- Buy pharmacy-brand extra strength antacid tablets instead of calcium glutonate tablets for the same source of calcium and save as much as $100 per year. (Take them with meals.) Replacing calcium glutamate tablets with Tums will save you money, too.

BUYER BEWARE

Buying medical insurance is difficult enough without having to worry about insurance scams—but scams have become more common recently, due to families and businesses trying to beat the rising costs of insurance. You may be getting taken if:

• **You're self-employed or own or work for a small business.** Because small business owners don't have the purchasing power of big companies, they often look for lower rates—and fake plans may seem to offer just what they want.

• **You have a preexisting condition that other insurers won't cover.** Your scam antenna should go up if the provider is strangely eager to offer you a policy, when others have declined.

• **You're looking for less expensive insurance.** Scammers may offer you below-rate coverage, a large provider network, or generous benefits. Shop around for several quotes from insurance firms you know, so you'll be able to spot a too-good-to-be-true policy.

So how do you prevent being scammed? Do your research. Call your state's insurance department (visit the National Association of Insurance Commissioners Web site at naic.org for information) to learn if your prospective insurer is licensed to do business in your state. If it's not, take a pass—it's operating illegally. (And do your research even if you're using an agent. Some agents knowingly sell fake plans, while others do so unintentionally because they didn't do their homework.)

- Buy vitamin C pills with plain ascorbic acid, not the more expensive (but not any more effective) pills with Ester-C or rosehips.

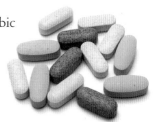

insurance plans

- Does your medical insurance cover glasses? If not, find out if your insurer and local opticians work together to offer discounts.

- Use a healthcare flex-plan if your employer offers it. You save by putting pre-tax dollars into the plan, which are then used to reimburse yourself for approved medical expenses. Be careful, though: you'll lose the money if you don't use it all by year's end.

- Does a mom need life insurance? According to conventional wisdom, if you're a stay-at-home mother, you don't need it because, should you die, your husband wouldn't have to replace your income. But many insurance experts are now challenging this assumption. If you answer yes to the following questions, you should consider at least a modest term life-insurance policy:

    1. If you have children and your husband had to pay for child care, could he afford it? Depending on the number and the ages of your kids, your family might need funds to cover this unexpected expense.

2. Are you planning to go back to work when the children are older? Lots of women do, in part to help cover the kids' college costs. Your husband would have to compensate for this future income, too.

3. Are you ineligible for social security benefits? You have to spend at least ten years in the workforce to be eligible; but if you are, your kids would be able to claim these benefits until they turn 18. This could make a life-insurance policy less important or even unnecessary. Many insurance firms encourage wives to get coverage through a rider on their husband's policy. But an individual policy could cost 50 percent less than a rider. You can find more information and policy price comparisons at term4sale.com, an independent Web site.

- Buy term life insurance—which ends at a particular time, such as an adult child's birthday—rather than whole life, which covers you until death. Term life insurance is cheaper.

homeowners' insurance

Homeowners' insurance rates seem to keep climbing, with no end in sight. Try these strategies keep your costs under control.

- Contact several agents when you're shopping for insurance. Even if your agent represents several insurers, he or she may not be able to give you the least expensive options.

- Don't automatically renew your policy. Different companies have different rates, so be sure to shop around for a less expensive policy before deciding to renew your current one.

- Raise your annual deductible. If you increase your deductible to $1,000 from $250, you can save up to 25 percent on your homeowners' policy. Since most policy holders make a claim only every eight to ten years, you'll save more in the long run by paying a lower premium.

- Install smoke and burglar alarms and get a discount. You can save as much as 20 percent on your insurance if you install approved sprinkler and fire alarm systems hooked up to an outside service. Keep in mind that these systems are expensive; you may not recoup these costs for a few years.

- Ask for any and all discounts. Some insurance companies offer lower premiums if you combine their homeowners' insurance with their auto insurance, while others cut rates for nonsmokers or people 55 and older.

credit

Credit cards can work in your favor—or against it,
depending on how savvy you are. Check out the following information about credit reports and credit
cards and save.

free credit reports

By law, you're entitled to one free copy of your credit
report annually from each of the three big credit bureaus
(Equifax, Experian, and TransUnion). And they will fulfill
that obligation at no charge—but only if you order from
the right Web site. Log on to the wrong one, and you may
wind up paying for costly services.

- The centralized site you want is annualcreditreport.com;
  there, you can order free reports from all three of the
  bureaus (or if you prefer, call toll-free: 877-322-8228). But
  be careful. There are sites with similar-sounding names,
  like freecreditreport.com, that attract customers with the
  promise of a free report, then push fee-based services like
  identity theft insurance or credit monitoring at a monthly
  cost ranging from $9.95 to $29.95. The credit bureau sites
  themselves also try to sell you packages.

- Are extra credit services worth buying? Monitoring does
  alert you to unusual activity on your credit report—but if

you don't like paying a monthly fee, you can use free reports to do your own periodic checkup (every four months, request a free report from a different bureau). Look for mistakes that can affect your credit score as well as evidence of identity theft.

- Once you place an order at annualcreditreport.com, the credit bureau you specified will mail you the document or let you download it. Check it carefully; if you find something wrong, contact the bureau and clear it up.

credit cards

- Pay your credit card bill on time and in full to avoid interest charges.

- If you are a good customer, you can ask the bank issuing your credit card to waive the annual fee.

- When you receive one of those offers in the mail for a low-interest credit card, call your credit card company and ask the customer service representative to reduce your rate to match the offer. Chances are good you'll get it.

- If you encounter the occasional late fee, always call your credit card company and ask for the fee to be waived. Often, the customer service rep will quickly agree (particularly if your payment history is solid).

entertainment

Entertainment costs can be low (renting DVDs to use at home) or high (attending live theater or sporting events), depending on what you choose to do. You can save money on all kinds of entertainment—both expensive and inexpensive—and best of all, you can find entertainment for free. Follow these tips for lots of low-cost fun.

books

If you're a bookworm, buying your reading fix can quickly become an expensive habit. Here are easy and inexpensive solutions to the problem.

- Swap books online that you've read for books you want— simply for the cost of shipping—at sites like bookins.com, paperbackswap.com, and bookmooch.com.

- If you can't find what you want on a book-swapping site, trying buying used books. The best places online for used books include well-known names like amazon.com and half.com. Try also sites like abebooks.com, addall.com, and bookfinder.com, search engines that find the books you want through used booksellers.

- Looking for used textbooks? Try amazon.com, abebooks.com, addall.com, and half.com. Bigwords.com is the best of the textbook-comparison-shopping sites; others include campusi.com and bookbyte.com.

- If you prefer buying used textbooks directly from other students (and selling yours to them), try the Book Exchange Network (tbxn.com). You can also post free ads for hard-to-find books.

- When publishers over-print a book, you get a bargain. You can usually find "remainders" for a steal at your local book-store or chain, and a terrific selection of bargain books (a.k.a. remainders) online at Daedalus Books & Music (daedalusbooks.com). Here you'll find thousands of books for up to 90 percent off the list price.

- Always look at the book selection of your warehouse club. You'll find great prices on adult and children's books, including bestsellers.

- The best way to save money on books is to take them out of the library. But if you just can't wait for a bestseller to show up on the shelves, try this trick: buy the book with a friend (preferably at a discount), and split the cost.

movies
and theater

Want to go out but don't want to spend a fortune?
Try the tips below for a night on the town.

movies

- Buy the annual Entertainment Book at your local library
  or school fundraiser (or buy it online at entertainment-
  book.com) for movie ticket discounts. Even after factor-
  ing in the cost of the book, you'll come out ahead if you
  and a friend go to the movies only six times a year.

- Make your AAA
  membership even
  more worthwhile by
  taking advantage of
  its discount movie
  tickets. You'll find
  offers to Clearview

  Cinemas, AMC, National Amusement and Regal Cinemas.

- Many local and national groups now offer discounted tickets as an additional membership benefit. The National
  Business Association (nationalbusiness.org), for example,
  gives members the opportunity to see non-matinee movies
  at matinee prices.

- Plenty of Web sites, like movieticketdiscounts.com, offer up to 35 percent discounts on movie tickets at over 1,000 theaters.

- Your ticket stub may be your ticket to a cheaper dinner. Restaurants near movie theaters occasionally give you a discount if you show your stub after the movie.

theater

- Plan your summer entertainment around free concerts and plays in local parks.

- Want to see live theater for free? Volunteer as an usher at your local theater.

- Most theaters—even Broadway theaters—offer cheap seats in the back. Find out how much they cost.

- Ask for standing room only tickets. You'll have a great view of the stage at a fraction of the cost of an orchestra seat.

GOING OUT ON THE TOWN?

• **Don't pay for a babysitter.** Instead, trade child care with a friend—but be sure to keep track of who babysits for how many hours.

• **Form a child care co-op with a group of friends.** Keep a log that records how many hours each member has babysat (credits) and how many hours each has used babysitting services (debits). You want a babysitter? Call the secretary (who changes every month), who will determine who has the largest time debit. The secretary gives you that name (or group of names); you then call to set up the babysitting date. The babysitter later calls the secretary to report the number of hours he or she sat for you. The secretary credits the babysitter that amount of time and debits you. The group sets a limit on the number of debit hours that members can accrue before they're no longer allowed babysitting services.

home entertainment

Staying home can save you big bucks over going out—but there are even ways to save on your home entertainment costs.

- Take videos and DVDs out of the library instead of buying them at the store. Some libraries also offer books on tape and on CD, music CDs, and video games.

- Join a movie-rental club like netflix.com or blockbuster.com. Go online, rent as many DVDs as you like, and receive them in the mail a few days later. Return them in postage-paid envelopes. You'll often spend less in time and money than if you went to your local video/DVD rental store.

- Buy your CDs, videos, and DVDs used—and start with amazon.com and half.com for low prices. Half.com offers you the choice of brand new, like new, very good, good, and acceptable, and sorts your choices by the final price (including shipping). Because it's a division of eBay, half.com even alerts you to relevant eBay auctions.

- Daedalus Books & Music (daedalusbooks.com) offers overstock CDs that can save you up to 90 percent.

- When's the best time—in terms of cost—to rent a movie? Tuesdays at 1:00—when video/DVD stores often offer midweek deals. By one o'clock, the morning returns will have been reshelved.

- Consider switching to basic cable and joining an online movie club for films you want to see rather than paying for hundreds of premium channels you probably don't watch.

- Sign up for deals on cable—two months of cable for half price, for example—and then cancel your subscription at the end of the offer. Keep track of when the deals expire on your calendar or in a tickler file.

- Which is the best TV service buy for you? If you want local programming, pick cable.

- Listen to the music you want when you want by visiting sites like youtube.com and pandora.com.

sports

Whether you and your children are playing sports or watching sports, you know it's going to cost a pretty penny. Here are ways to make those pennies (and dollars) go further.

sports gear

- Check out annual gear swaps held by many local sports organizations.

- Find retailers who sell secondhand sports equipment. You can save 25 to 75 percent off retail prices of new ice skates, ski boots, and more at Play It Again Sports, a franchise that also lets you trade in old items for cash or credit toward store purchases in the future. (Find the store nearest you at playitagainsports.com.) Make sure that the equipment is in good condition with no cracks or pieces missing.

- Take advantage of the Internet: some sites sell used sports gear. Try the outlet section of Fogdog Sports (fogdog.com) for reduced prices. Fogdog also offers great off-season deals; for example, you'll find heavily discounted ski pants on the site in the summer months. Other helpful sites include ebay.com, ubid.com, gearbay.com, and outdoorreview.com. Again, confirm that the equipment is in proper shape.

- Call sports stores that specialize in one sport; many have a trade-in program. Bicycle repair shops and retailers often do this, for example, and the bikes they sell may have been refurbished and professionally road tested.

- Safety and protective gear—such as helmets, eyewear, and undergarment padding—should not be bought secondhand.

sporting events

- Attend minor league games. You'll pay less than at the pro stadium and probably get better seating, too.

- Go to college games if you can. You may see future stars playing, and you can't beat the price.

- Don't buy food or souvenirs at the game. The cost of your attendance will go through the roof.

photography

You've bought your new digital camera and even fig-
ured out how to use it. Now you're starting to print
out your photos—but wait! Your printer may not be
the penny-wise way to go. Once you factor in photo-
quality paper and ink, you may be spending as much
as sixty cents on a single photo. So what should
you do?

- Check out online photo developing sites like snapfish.com
  and shutterfly.com. (Be sure to comparison shop; some
  sites charge twice as much as others.) You may have to pay
  for shipping charges, but standard shipping could cost
  less than $2 for 25 or fewer photos, so you will still come
  out ahead.

- If you're not wild about having your photographs shipped
  to you, check out mass merchandisers like Target or
  Wal-Mart and warehouse clubs like Costco. They offer
  reasonable to good deals on printing. You simply upload
  your digital pictures to their Web site, and pick up your
  prints at your nearest store. You can also upload your
  photos at the store. You'll spend fifteen to fifty nine cents
  per photo, depending on the number of prints that you
  order.

special events

Whether you're buying gifts for a birthday, wrapping a Christmas present, hosting a dinner party, or decorating for Halloween, special events are even more special when you save on everything from gift wrap to flowers. Here are money-saving ways to particularly enjoy the special events in your life.

gifts

- Shop at after-Christmas sales for next year's birthday and Christmas presents.

- When shopping for a present, buy two gifts at once if you find a buy one, get one free (or buy one, get one half off) sale. Put the second one away until you need it.

- Buy gifts in bulk if you find a great sale on a timeless gift like a wallet.

- Use coupons, rebates, rewards programs, and other money-saving strategies (see page 8) when buying gifts.

- Don't forget the benefits of online shopping (save time and money on sale items), especially if shipping is free. (See page 27 for more online shopping tips.)

- If your gift is to take the recipient to a meal at a restaurant, be sure to celebrate at lunch rather than pricier dinner.

- Make your own food gifts: cookie mix in a jar, mulled wine, or caramel popcorn.

- Buy hostess gifts like wine in bulk, especially around the holidays.

- When sending party guests home with a small gift, consider inexpensive favors like balloons, homemade goodies such as your special cookies, small flowering plants, and, in autumn, tiny jack-o'-lanterns.

- Create the perfect inexpensive present by filling a pretty basket or box with items your friend or family member will love. You can often find containers (and, if you're lucky, fragrant lotions and other pampering products) on sale; assembling the gift basket yourself can save you a fortune over pre-packaged gift baskets.

gift wrap and cards

- Buy next year's holiday gift wrap, bows, and ribbons at this year's after-Christmas sales. You may even be able to buy solid-colored wrap or wrap with a nonholiday theme to use for other occasions—such as birthdays—throughout the year.

- Use maps you no longer need for gift wrap.

- Try wrapping a child's present in newspaper comics for a fun and funny effect.

BUYER BEWARE

Gift cards can be wonderful presents for the giver and the receiver: the giver doesn't have the pressure of finding the perfect present, and the receiver gets to buy exactly what he or she wants. But both giver and receiver need to know that hidden fees and other restrictions can reduce the value of the gift card. Here's what should be on your radar:

• **Expiration dates.** Some gift cards come with a date by which you must spend the entire value of the card. This is a "use-it-or-lose-it" situation.

• **Inactivity fees.** Your gift card may not expire, but you may be charged fees if you don't use it within a specified period of time.

• **Unredeemed dollars.** If you don't spend the full value of your card when you purchase an item, the retailer may not give you cash for the balance. Retailers don't have to give you the difference in cash—in fact, they make a lot of money with this tactic—but many will if you ask.

• **Lost cards.** Write down the identification number of the gift card and keep it in a safe place in case you lose your card. You'll need that number and/or the receipt for it when you try to get a refund or another card.

- Save for future use decorative gift bags, tissue paper, and gift wrap you receive with presents.

- Shop for next year's holiday cards during after-Christmas sales. You'll find great deals.

- Use the front of last year's Christmas cards for this year's gift tags.

- Buy gift cards in packages, rather than individually. You can find packs of blank cards as well as cards with multiple greetings at warehouse clubs, craft stores, and discount stores.

- Send online greetings to save postage.

- Use software to design your own cards.

flowers

- Stretch your flower dollars with these tips:

    1. Keep flower arrangements out of bright light; they will last longer this way.

    2. Change the water every day.

    3. Add an aspirin to the water to lengthen the life of the flowers, or add ½ cup of seltzer or carbonated water and 1 teaspoon sugar to the water.

- Watch out for shipping, delivery, and handling charges when ordering flowers over the Internet or via toll-free phone numbers. They can add up fast. FTD, for example, charges quite a bit extra for delivery on a Saturday. Instead, visit cheapflowers.com for plenty of pretty bouquets at reasonable prices—including many for $35.

- Check your local warehouse store for inexpensive flowers.

- Grow your own flowers.

holiday decorations

- Buy holiday decorations right after that particular holiday—you'll find great deals on Halloween costumes on November 1 and Christmas ornaments on December 26.

- Buy holiday-themed decorations that aren't sold as holiday decorations—like heart stickers for Valentine's  Day—when you see them on sale throughout the year.

- Save all your decorations instead of buying new ones for the following year. For example, keep reusable centerpieces, streamers, window clings, and door decorations and you'll save a bundle.

- Organize your decorations so you'll know what you've saved (and what you won't need to buy). Keep decorations for each holiday separate.

- Inexpensive, small decorations make a big difference. Change your tablecloth or placemats, front door wreath, or mantel decorations with each holiday.

- Make your own holiday decorations. Check online, in books, and in magazines (including *Good Housekeeping*) for ideas for easy, inexpensive decorations.

- To find out if energy-efficient holiday lights cut costs, the Good Housekeeping Research Institute recently tested five brands against a traditional set. It turns out the energy-efficient strands, or LED lights, used 85 to 90 percent less power than the standard ones. In bill-slashing terms: If you light a string of 50 LED bulbs for eight hours a day for one month straight, you'd save 50 cents per strand. That's not much if you hang just a few strings, but if you swirl lights around every shrub, the savings add up (use 20 strands and save $10).

travel

One of the best parts about traveling is anticipation—looking forward to seeing many new places and having new experiences. One of the worst parts is dreading the cost involved. Here are ways to get around that.

hotels

Invest some time searching for the best deal on hotels.

- Big hotel chains are trying to get you to book rooms through their Web sites—and your pocketbook can benefit from their efforts. For example, Wyndham recently offered a free night during your stay if you found a lower price than Wyndham offered on its Web site, and Hyatt took 20 percent off the lowest price you could find on the Internet for one of their rooms.

- Keep in mind that not all hotel Web sites or 800 numbers offer the best deal. Call the hotel directly; the hotel manager or desk clerk often has the authority to negotiate the price of the room depending on how booked the hotel is for that particular night.

- Call your hotel every week or so after you've booked your room. If rooms are still available or a block of rooms has been canceled, you may get a lower price.

- Check out Rewards Network (rewardsnetwork.com). Join the program for $49 a year and register a credit or debit card on the site. When you use that particular card at one of thousands of participating hotels, up to 5 percent of the room rate will be credited to your next credit or debit card statement.

- Do you want a bigger room for the price you've paid for your current room? Check in, then call the front desk around 9:00 PM, after most guests have arrived, and ask if you can upgrade.

- Hotels that cater to businesses can find themselves with empty rooms on weekends, which works to a bargain-hunter's advantage. Check chains like Ramada and Hilton for special weekend programs—and rates.

- Try booking your hotel room on Sunday. Reservations clerks are eager to fill up rooms, and the business folks aren't around to discourage deals.

- Hotel brokers can save you a bundle—up to 70 percent off the rate the hotel may have quoted you. Check out Hotel Reservations Network (1-800-96-HOTELS) and usahotelguide.com.

- Hostels are a great, inexpensive alternative to hotels, even for families (just ask for a private room). You have your choice of more than 4,000 hostels in 60 countries via Hostelling International USA (hiusa.org).

- Looking for a deal on a fancy resort? Think Florida in the summer. Gulf breezes help counteract

the heat of June and early July, when resort hotels slash
their rates.

- Always ask the hotel reservations agent for discounts.
  Ask for a AAA rate if you belong to the auto club. Or
  see if there's an Entertainment Book rate—you'll more
  than recoup the cost of the book with only one or two
  nights' stay.

SAVE WHILE YOU SLEEP

If you like the price of camping but hate crashing on
the ground, try towable pop-up campers. With rates
starting at $40 per day, they're almost as inexpensive
as tents—but a lot more
comfortable. Up to
eight people can
sleep, cook, and dine
in these units, which
have mesh sides to let in
the fresh air.

When it's time to hit the road, the sides collapse
into a lightweight trailer that can be towed by a mid-
size car. Find a rental near you at getrv.com.

planes

Planes, trains, and automobiles may be your alternatives for modes of travel, and planes are undoubtedly the most expensive. Here's how to save on this major travel expense.

- If you want to keep up with the latest airfares, or know when a price drops to a level you'd like, sign up for an e-mail alert.

  1. farecompare.com e-mails prices on flights between your home city and key locales, or between any two cities you choose. The alerts are sent up to four hours before fares are published online or to agents.

  2. cheaptickets.com lets you specify nonstop or weekend flights.

  3. expedia.com's Fare Alerts are easy to get: You register and download an icon to your desktop; double click on it to see the current fare.

- Try kayak.com when searching for bargain airfares. After you provide your travel destination and your ideal vacation dates, Kayak whips out a Best Fare History table showing exactly how the price has moved over the past several weeks. Then you can decide whether to book or perhaps wait a little while, in the hopes that the price will eventually drop to your liking.

- Always go directly to the airline's Web site to check ticket prices. It often offers Web-exclusive discounts, and you can avoid paying the booking fee other sites charge. Plus, some discount airlines like Southwest sell online tickets only on their own sites.

- When's the best time to book a flight? Try Wednesdays at 1:00 AM. The cycle of rising fares starts on Fridays, then heads back down on Wednesday, and the 24-hour window to buy is reloaded right after midnight.

- Surprised that you now have to pay for snacks on your flight? Lots of airlines charge hefty prices for snacks and meals onboard, and some have discontinued food service altogether. Here are some easy, inexpensive take-along suggestions:

  1. Berries, oranges, and grapes. They are yummy and keep you hydrated. Cracker Barrel Cheddar cheese, which comes in a convenient one-ounce size, adds protein and goes great with fruit.

  2. Crunchy veggies (baby carrots, celery, fennel, green and red peppers). They are especially satisfying when you're enduring long delays. Want to dip them in hummus? Sabra now sells individual-size containers.

  3. Whole wheat crackers or pita bread. They complete the feast.

rental cars

Renting a car can give you sticker shock, particularly in large cities. Try these tips to drive away with a bargain.

- Don't pick up your rental car at the airport. It can cost almost 25 percent more than picking it up at another location. Try taking an airport shuttle to a city hotel, where you're likely to find branches of car rental companies. Even with the cost of the shuttle, you'll come out ahead.

- Why pay twice for auto insurance when you rent a car? If you own a car, you probably don't need to buy rental insurance. If your insurance policy covers you for supplemental liability insurance (SLI), which protects you in case of damage to property or injury to others, and collision, you won't need either SLI or a collision damage waver (CDW). Both can add substantial amounts to your rental car cost. In addition, many credit cards give you CDW coverage if you use your card to rent the car and decline coverage offered by the rental agency.

- Always fill the gas tank of your rental car before you return it. If you don't, you may get charged a hefty price per gallon, and/or you may be charged for a full tank even if the tank was half full.

- You can often find special rates—or upgrades—for rental cars if you book online.

- Always mention your AAA membership when you rent a car; it can save you up to 20 percent.

- Mention your warehouse club membership when you rent a car. You may get a discount.

- Check the Entertainment Book (entertainmentbook.com) for car rental coupons.

cruises

Set sail with big savings when you plan for your cruise with these tips in mind.

- Cruise passengers—typically those who booked early or travel on the cruise line often—can get upgraded to a nicer cabin if the cruise fails to sell out its costlier cabins. Have your travel agent ask for an upgrade.

- Find cruise bargains—up to 50 percent off the going rate—at cruisesonly.com. You'll also find helpful passenger reviews.

- Be flexible with your cruise date and save. You may find that shifting your departure date by a week will save your family hundreds of dollars.

vacation strategies

With high gas prices and exorbitant airfare, your dream vacation may look like . . . just a dream. But with these tips, you can swing the trip of a lifetime.

- Plan vacations around visits with family and friends to save on food and lodging.

- The typical American family spends an average of $3,700 on a two-week driving trip. That's a nice piece of change—which could pay off your credit card bill or swell your savings. Skipping the annual getaway may sound harsh, but staying home for a change can actually be a treat. The trick is doing fun stuff in your own neighborhood. A few possibilities:

1. Pursue something you've thought about but have never had time for. Take sailing lessons, start learning Italian, buy watercolors and an easel. Whatever your fantasy, it's probably cheaper than a trip.

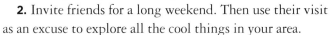

2. Invite friends for a long weekend. Then use their visit as an excuse to explore all the cool things in your area.

3. Eat out every day at a different restaurant. You'll spend only a fraction of what you would on a vacation.

4. Mellow out for a week. Pick a time when the kids have no summer activities scheduled. Then sleep late, hang out at the community pool, catch lightning bugs at dusk, play Marco Polo, and most important, don't hurry.

5. Take a quirky overnight trip. One example: At a local state park, rent a yurt—a cross between a tent and a tepee—for a night or two.

• Book for the off-season. If you travel when everyone else doesn't, you can find lodging for half what you'd pay during peak times. Airfare is often cheaper, too.

1. Try Orlando in early summer. Temperatures in May and June are still pleasant, and a Disney vacation becomes more affordable when you can save on hotels and flights.

2. Vacation in Europe in April, May, or September. You'll find lovely weather, fewer tourists, and best of all, lower fares. (Avoid August, when Europeans are taking their vacations.)

3. Travel to the Caribbean in May. It's warm, rates are cheaper than they are in winter, and hurricane season doesn't start until June.

- Wait. Procrastination may pay off when you're trying to rent a house for part of the summer. If you haven't signed up for a rental by late June or July, you may find that owners are desperate to rent out their empty houses—and will drop their rents in order to make a deal.

  Here's how to get a good place at the last minute:

  1. Be flexible. You probably can't get the ocean view *and* the pool *and* the Jacuzzi with the underwater light show. List your priorities.

  2. Check out Web sites listing last-minute rentals, like lastminuteusvacations.com.

  3. Call local agents. If you start chatting, one might tell you about a new place that hasn't been listed yet, or put you on the list of people to notify if there's a cancellation. Also, ask if the agent knows of owners who use their properties only on weekends. Maybe you can rent one on weekdays.

  4. Search classifieds. Some owners still list their vacancies in newspapers, so if you can, visit the vacation spot and pick up a copy of the local paper.

  5. Call colleges in the area. Faculty members often rent out their homes while they're away on summer research trips.

6. Consider doing a home exchange. Scan Web sites like homeexchange.com and intervac.com for families looking to vacation in your city or region. Then contact one to explore making a swap.

7. Look for super-last-minute rentals. Vacation rental sites like homeaway.com may offer discounted rates from motivated owners who've had a renter suddenly cancel.

● Search the Web . . . in the right places. Use the top travel Web sites to your advantage with these tricks:

1. expedia.com Find your perfect hotel by searching by theme (family hotels, beach hotels, all-inclusive hotels, and so on). Then click on the Activities section to buy advance tickets for local attractions at no extra cost, and get the added advantage of skipping those long lines when you visit.

2. travelzoo.com This site lists the best values on hotels, airlines, rental-car agencies, and cruise lines from more than 300 companies. You can sign up for e-mail alerts to the Internet's best travel deals of the week and regional bargain information.

3. vrbo.com This vacation rental by owner site, with listings in predominantly popular family travel destinations, helps you find a vacation house or condo rental.

● Big clearinghouses may not always list the best deals. You're sometimes better off looking for specials on individual hotel or airline Web sites. It'll mean a little more surfing, but the effort can really pay off.

- One great way to save money is by getting advice from people who've already taken the trip. That's where forums and reviews come in.

   1. tripadvisor.com and **frommers.com** are the best for leisure travelers. Trip Advisor is info-rich, covering hotels, restaurants, tourist attractions, and other venues in thousands of locations.

   2. caribbeanhotdeals.com and **kayak.com** forums have sections just for the money-conscious. Kayak also provides current fares for any destination in its postings.

   3. orbitz.com offers real-time updates from travelers. You'll get the latest information about security wait lines, taxi lines, parking, traffic, and more.

- When looking for a vacation bargain, why enter your travel search criteria again and again on site after site? A meta-search engine saves time by trolling multiple travel sites for you. And it won't clutter your e-mail in-box with unwanted trip suggestions. Mobissimo.com and sidestep.com check hundreds of sites, including those of airlines, hotels, travel agencies, and trip packagers.

- Rent a house instead of a room. Many resort areas have condos, villas, or houses available at daily or weekly rates—and their per-night prices often work out to be lower than those of area hotels. Plus, you get lots of extras,

BUYER BEWARE

While surfing the Web for travel savings, be sure to:

Read the fine print. Find out if all fees and taxes are included in the cost, and whether weekend travel is excluded from the price.

Compare deals with booking directly from airlines or hotels. Many travel sites charge booking fees; to avoid them, reserve from the Web site of the airline or hotel.

Consider packages, but be cautious; it may cost less if you pay separately for your flights, hotel, and car rental.

Don't delay if you see an e-mail special. It may not have a long shelf life.

Be on the lookout for bogus write-ups when you're reading online forums and postings. Traveler reviews can be easily fudged. The reviews are more likely to be genuine if they include detailed trip reports and statements like "things might have been better if . . . "

like a full kitchen, multiple bathrooms, and a washer and dryer. Condos usually include resort-style amenities like swimming pools and tennis courts. Search homeaway.com and cyberrentals.com for available properties in popular destinations. To avoid surprises on your bill, don't book until you've asked about cleaning fees, pet fees, security deposits, and applicable room taxes.

- Save on meals. A kitchenette can save you a bundle. Another trick: book hotels that include free breakfasts or afternoon snacks. That can easily save you $20 to $30 a day.

- Make the most of package deals. Airfare-and-lodging combos are easy to find, but you may be less aware of the many other discounts in hotel packages, which often offer lower-priced tickets to popular nearby attractions as part of the room rate. You can find these combos on the convention-and-visitors' Web site for the city or state you're visiting.

- Check the local tourism board Web site. You may find discount passes that get you into several attractions for one low price.

CLIP AND SAVE

By the time you hunt down the picture-perfect frames for your family's vacation photos, that road trip will be a distant memory. Instead, put everyone's favorite prints on immediate display with cheerful, cut-rate holders. They're a snap to create—all you need are brightly colored binder clips and white card stock (at craft stores). Affix photographs to card stock with an acid-free glue stick, then trace a one-inch border on all sides with a ruler. Cut out, and prop in the clips.

- Check out visitors' bureaus before you visit. You can get the best specific information about your destination from city and state visitors' bureaus—for free. If you ask, these bureaus will send you kits that detail area hotels, restaurants, and events. Search the Web by typing in your destination and the words "visitors bureau" or "chamber of commerce."

- Pick up a CityPass when you visit one of ten urban areas for big discounts on that city's most popular attractions. This card can save you up to 50 percent of the price of individually purchased tickets to the same number of attractions. The New York CityPass, for example, costs $65; you would spend $130 if you paid for each attraction separately. New York sites include the Empire State Building Observatory, the Metropolitan Museum of Art, the Museum of Modern Art, the Guggenheim Museum, the American Museum of Natural History, and a Circle Line Sightseeing Cruise—plus a discount at Bloomingdale's and 12 New York restaurants. You can

buy a CityPass in Atlanta, Boston, Chicago, Hollywood, New York, Philadelphia, San Francisco, Seattle, Southern California, and Toronto. Visit citypass.com for more information.

- Make the visitors' bureau of your destination your first in-person vacation stop. Most offer discounts on local attractions that you may not have heard about in your pre-vacation research.

cars

A car is a vital part of most households, and a major expense as well. But if you follow the tips in this section you'll save on buying, leasing, and maintaining it as well as on gas and insurance.

buying
and selling cars

Whether you're buying a new or used car, or selling one, you need to know strategies for saving money. These tips let you do exactly that.

when you're buying new:

1 Window-shop first. To compare models and narrow down your choices, check out edmunds.com for information on mileage, safety rating, price, and features.

2 Kick the tires. After you've selected your favorites, head to the dealer for a test-drive. But don't get sucked into negotiating, even if you fall in love with a car.

3 Get the real story on prices. After your test-drive, go back to edmunds.com and look up the true market value, which is what a particular model is selling for in your area. Use this information to determine what you're willing to pay.

4 Make a deal. Log on to carsdirect.com and edmunds.com and plug in the model you want and your zip code. Dealers in

the area who are affiliated with the sites will negotiate with you. Some dealers will even deliver the car. With others, you'll have to pick it up.

5 Buy a new car on August 31. That's when vacations and back-to-school errands leave car lots deserted, with new models on the way. Also, dealers may be generous if they haven't met monthly quotas.

when you're buying used:

1 Search online for vehicles. Log on to sites like autonation.com, autotrader.com, carmax.com, cars.com, and craigslist.org, which let you shop by geographic location or zip code.

STAY IN CONTROL

Whether you're buying a new or used car, keep these tips in mind:

• **Don't fall in love.** Resist the temptation to look at cars outside your price range. And if the dealer's final offer isn't low enough, walk away.

• **Don't agree to expensive add-ons.** Beware of pitches from automobile dealers for loan-repayment insurance, antitheft devices, and any other extra features that you may not really need.

2 Prepare for your price negotiation. Check the Edmunds (edmunds.com), Kelley Blue Book (kbb.com), and Black Book (blackbookusa.com) sites to find out the value of the used car you're interested in. Edmunds also lists actual prices that people have paid for specific models.

3 Check the car's title. Once you've made a choice, order a particular vehicle's history report from autocheck.com or carfax.com. You may uncover problems in the car's history.

4 Don't forget to ask for repair records. It's important to know a car's past before you commit yourself.

WHO KNEW?

If you're buying a used car but hate haggling, try these strategies:

• **Shop at Car Max (carmax.com),** the nation's largest used-car chain (with locations in 22 states). CarMax's salespeople earn a flat fee for each model sold, so they have no incentive to tempt you with a more expensive vehicle. And the stores have a five-day money-back guarantee as well as a 30-day limited guarantee.

• **You can also buy without negotiating** at hertzcarsales.com, enterprisecarsales.com, and Enterprise sales locations, where manufacturers' warranties are often still in effect.

5 Buy on a weekday morning. Evenings and weekends bring heavy traffic, making it harder to haggle.

6 Look for good condition "fleet vehicles"—used cars that have been owned by salespeople or car-rental agencies—for a good deal.

when you're selling:

1 Know the market. Check autotrader.com to find out how many models like yours are on the used-car market in your area and what they're going for. This will help you set a price.

2 Advertise everywhere. List your car on sites like autotrader.com, carsdirect.com, and ebay.com—any that let buyers search by zip code.

3 Planning to keep your car for six years? Hold onto it for seven. In fact, if you keep every car you own for one year longer than you originally planned, you could save the equivalent of a whole car over your lifetime.

leasing cars

Leasing a car rather than buying one has its advantages, such as lower monthly payments and easy trade-ins. But you can also be blindsided by unexpected expenses. If you're planning to lease, follow these tips.

- Don't accept a lease without doing research. Before going to the dealer, visit leasewizard.com to find market lease costs for the car you want. If the dealer offers terms that are high, politely decline and ask for better ones.

- Don't get an open-end lease. That's one where the amount you'll owe for depreciation is the difference between the residual value and whatever the market value turns out to be when the lease is up. A closed-end lease is better because you and the dealer agree beforehand on what you'll owe.

- Don't skimp on the mileage allowance. Leases are typically based on driving 12,000 miles a year and require you to pay a whopping eight to twenty cents per extra mile when the lease expires. If you think you'll drive more, buy extra mileage up front; you might pay five cents a mile.

- Don't lease for longer than the warranty. Stretching the lease can lower payments, but if you need big repairs once the warranty runs out, you'll pay for them.

- Try not to buy gap insurance through the dealer. This coverage would pay the difference between the value of your car at the time it's stolen or destroyed and the residual value plus what you still owe on the lease. It may be cheaper to buy gap from your car insurer.

- Don't keep the car longer than you want. If you need to get out of your lease, advertise on leasetrader.com for $79.95. When a buyer takes over the lease, the seller pays leasetrader.com $249.95 and the buyer pays the site $149.95.

gas

Putting gas in your car can be financially painful. Here are ways to make filling up hurt a little less.

- Take the pedal off the medal and save. You can get 15 percent better fuel economy by driving at 55 miles per hour instead of 65 miles per hour.

- Keep your tires inflated to their recommended pressure. (Find this information on your car door or in your glove compartment and in your owner's manual.) The right pressure can improve your gas mileage by 3 percent.

- Avoid a rooftop carrier. If you use one, your fuel economy will plummet by about 5 percent.

- The best way to save gas? Walk or bike for your short errands. You'll use less gas—no gas!—and burn calories in the process.

- Replace filters on a regular basis.

- Get a new oxygen sensor; it can boost your mileage by up to 40 percent.

- Boost your fuel economy by getting regular wheel alignments. Check your owner's manual for the recommended intervals.

- Fill 'er up for less at your local Sam's, Costco, or BJ's Wholesale Club. These warehouse clubs generally charge four to ten cents less per gallon than regular gas stations.

- Find inexpensive gas online. Visit Web sites that list gas stations with the lowest prices in your area. Just enter your zip code to find the bargain pumps near you. Sites to try:

    1. automotive.com/gas-prices This site has an easy-to-read price chart, with the lowest rate for each gas grade—

regular, plus, premium, and diesel—clearly flagged by a bright color.

2. gaspricewatch.com You can filter the results by time, so if you're not interested in prices that are more than a day old, you can eliminate them from your search.

3. gasbuddy.com Besides checking out current costs, you can visit the Historical Price Chart to see how fuel rates in your state have fluctuated over time.

4. gaswatch.info and **fueleconomy.gov** and your local government's Web site, which may have gas pricing information, too.

- Keep your eyes open for gas stations that offer discounts on certain days of the week.

- Resist the temptation to top off your gas tank; the extra gas usually either spills or evaporates, so you'll just be wasting your money.

- Gas stations usually offer three grades of gasoline—regular, super or premium, and an in-between grade often called extra. Regular gas typically has an octane rating of 87, extra has 89, and super has 91 or higher. Use the least expensive grade that lets your car run without pinging (also called spark knock), which sounds like ball bearings being poured into a metal can. See what your owner's manual says.

- Sign up for a gas company credit card and get a rebate on the gas you buy.

service

Keep your car running well and you'll keep extra money in your pocket. Here's how to save on service.

- Stick to the basics at quick-serve lube shops to save your hard-earned money.
These franchises are good for oil changes, wiper fluid fill-ups, and checking tire pressure, but pressure you for extra services. Here's what to avoid:

    1. An engine flush (or oil flush). You don't need this unless you haven't been changing your oil as directed or if your car has more than 100,000 miles on it.

    2. A fuel injection system cleaning. Your car doesn't need this on a regular basis. Your certified auto mechanic will tell you if you have a clogged fuel injector.

    3. Coolant and transmission-fluid changes. Lube shops tend to oversell these. Again, your mechanic will tell you if you need them.

- One of the hardest decisions you'll have to make as a car owner is when you should stop fixing your old car and buy a new one. Here are some guidelines that can help you decide:

    1. Check your mileage. If you've maintained your car the way the manufacturer recommends, you can put on 150,000 miles before you'll need to replace it.

REPAIR AND SAVE

Cracks in the driveway may seem to be a problem that can be ignored, but if you don't fix them the cracks will get bigger and will be harder to repair. In addition, if they're near the house, moisture may seep into your foundation—creating a bigger, more expensive problem. Try these simple solutions to stop a complicated problem from developing.

• **Easy fix:** Remove loose debris and spray the area with a hose. Apply a crack filler designed for asphalt and allow it to dry thoroughly.

• **Pro tip:** If the cracks are deep, fill them with sand, then use the filler for the last quarter inch.

2. How much is your car worth? Check edmunds.com to determine your car's market value. Then have a certified mechanic inspect it to see if any parts will cause you problems in the short-term. If you're facing a $2,000 repair bill and your car is worth $4,000, you may want to ditch the old car.

3. How much has your car cost you over the past year? Add up every repair (but not routine maintenance, like an oil change) and compare it to the cost of a new car, which will run you several hundred dollars a month on average every year. If you keep your car, start a fund specifically for repairs, and be sure to have these repairs done by mechanics who offer warranties.

WINTERIZING SAVINGS

You know that you need to get your car ready for the winter months, but should you bother paying to winterize your car?

• **The Good Housekeeping Research Institute says** you should go to the garage if your battery is more than two years old. The mechanic will perform a "load" test—starting the car under simulated cold-weather conditions—which will tell you if you need a new battery.

• **Also, make sure your tire treads** are at least $\frac{1}{16}$ inch thick so your tires will perform well in snow and other wintery conditions. You can ask your mechanic to test your treads or test them yourself with a penny. Stick a penny head first into the tread grooves. If you can see the top of Lincoln's hair, the tread is worn and you need to replace the tire.

• **Unless you live in an extreme climate,** don't bother changing your oil to a winter weight oil.

• **If you live in a wintery location,** buy winter weight wiper blades and ask your auto-supply store to install them for free.

4. Think seriously about safety features. Does your current car have side air bags? Daytime running lights? If you're missing these features and they matter to you and your family, you may want to replace your car.

5. Stress and aggravation factors. Will taking your car to the mechanic more often than in the past make you berserk?

Will you worry that your car will break down at the most inopportune time, perhaps on a long-distance trip? You need to factor your emotional health into your car-keeping or -buying decision.

- Consider renting a car for long trips rather than driving an older model. You may save on costly repairs.

insurance

Car insurance is essential. Here are ways to save on this often expensive must-have.

- If you stick close to home when driving, ask your insurance agent about a "recreational use" policy. It's designed for those who rarely drive out of their neighborhoods and can save you 10 percent or more on your insurance policy.

- Take a defensive driving class. (The AARP and driving schools offer them.) Your diploma can save you up to 10 percent on your insurance premiums.

- Compare your current auto policy with others before you renew, since identical coverage can vary wildly in price from company to company. Visit Progressive Auto Insurance (progressive.com) to compare your policy to those from other companies and potentially save hundreds of dollars.

- Raise your annual deductible. If you boost your deductible from $200 to $500, you can save up to 30 percent on your collision and comprehensive auto coverage.

- Ask for discounts for:
    1. Multiple policies
    2. Cars with antitheft devices
    3. Drivers with no accidents or speeding violations

- Either drop or reduce the comprehensive and collision coverage part of your car insurance if your auto has entered its golden years. If your insurance premiums are at least 10 percent of your car's market value, get rid of that particular coverage.

- Unless you use AAA for its discounts at hotels and area attractions, you may want to reconsider your membership. Your insurance company—or even your cell phone provider—may offer roadside assistance for substantially less.

index

photo credits

Courtesy of Amy's Organic: 80

James Baigrie: 117

Ila Duncan: 14, 207

GE 7.5' Just Cut Fraser Fir: 191

Steve J. Benbow/Getty Images: 211

Charles Maraia/Getty Images: 99

Steve Giralt: 175

Gregor Halenda: 57, 65

Jupiter Images: 193

LuckyOliver: 38, 67, 143, 159, 164, 178

Charles Maraia: 66

Andrew McCaul: 55, 69

PhotoObjects: 74, 88, 95, 103, 105, 125-127, 133, 135, 156, 160, 198, 216, 220 (top)

Mark Platt: 77, 150

Punchstock: 10, 51

Marc Royce: 137

David Turner/Studio D: 139, 150

Steve Wisbauer/Getty Images: 1, 3

All remaining imagery: iStockphoto

Copyright © 2008 by Hearst Communications, Inc.

Every effort has been made to ensure that all the information in this book is accurate at the time of its printing. Please note, however, that some Web site addresses and content may have changed since then.

Library of Congress Cataloging-in-Publication Data
Good housekeeping : good deals & smart steals : save money on everything! / from editors of Good Housekeeping magazine.
   p. cm.
 Includes index.
 ISBN 978-1-58816-690-6
1. Consumer education. 2. Shopping. I. Good housekeeping. II. Title: Good deals & smart steals : save money on everything! III. Title: Good deals and smart steals : save money on everything!
TX335.G62 2008
 640.73—dc22

            2008008673

10 9 8 7 6 5 4 3 2 1

Book design by Elizabeth Van Itallie

The Good Housekeeping Seal is a concise statement of the *Good Housekeeping* Consumers' Policy: If a product bearing the Seal proves to be defective within two years of purchase, *Good Housekeeping* will replace the product or refund the purchase price. For more information go to www.goodhousekeeping.com.

Published by Hearst Books
A Division of Sterling Publishing Co., Inc.
387 Park Avenue South, New York, NY 10016

Good Housekeeping and Hearst Books are trademarks of Hearst Communications, Inc.

www.goodhousekeeping.com

For information about custom editions, special sales, premium and corporate purchases, please contact Sterling Special Sales Department at 800-805-5489 or specialsales@sterlingpublishing.com.

Distributed in Canada by Sterling Publishing
c/o Canadian Manda Group, 165 Dufferin Street
Toronto, Ontario, Canada M6K 3H6

Distributed in Australia by Capricorn Link (Australia) Pty. Ltd.
P.O. Box 704, Windsor, NSW 2756 Australia

Manufactured in China

Sterling ISBN 978-1-58816-690-6